The Poetry Book

Poems for children

chosen by
Fiona Waters

Decorations by
Caroline Crossland

Dolphin

Contents

SUN, MOON, STARS

FROM AN OMAHA CEREMONY FOR THE NEWBORN

Sun, moon, stars,
You that move in the heavens,
Hear this mother!
A new life has come among you.
Make its life smooth.

VIRGINIA DRIVING HAWK SNEVE

FAIR ROSA

Fair Rosa was a lovely child
a lovely child   a lovely child
fair Rosa was a lovely child
a long time ago

a wicked fairy cast a spell
cast a spell   cast a spell
a wicked fairy cast a spell
a long time ago

fair Rosa slept for a hundred years
a hundred years   a hundred years
fair Rosa slept for a hundred years
a long time ago

the hedges they all grew around
grew around   grew around
the hedges they all grew around
a long time ago

a handsome prince came ariding by
riding by   riding by
a handsome prince came ariding by
a long time ago

he cut the hedges one by one
one by one   one by one
he cut the hedges one by one
a long time ago

he kissed fair Rosa's lilywhite hand
lilywhite hand   lilywhite hand
he kissed fair Rosa's lilywhite hand
a long time ago

fair Rosa will not sleep no more
sleep no more   sleep no more
fair Rosa will not sleep no more
a long time ago

ANONYMOUS

THE RAILWAY CHILDREN

When we climbed the slopes of the cutting
We were eye-level with the white cups
Of the telegraph poles and the sizzling wires.

Like lovely freehand they curved for miles
East and miles west beyond us, sagging
Under their burden of swallows.

We were small and thought we knew nothing
Worth knowing. We thought words travelled the wires
In the shiny pouches of raindrops,

Each one seeded full with the light
Of the sky, the gleam of the lines, and ourselves
So infinitesimally scaled

We could stream through the eye of a needle.

SEAMUS HEANEY

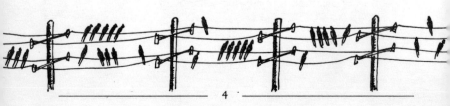

THE BOY WHO DROPPED LITTER

'ANTHONY WRIGGLY
SHAME ON YOU!'
screeched the teacher
as she spotted him
scrunching up his crisp packet
and dropping it carefully
on to the pavement outside school.

'If everyone went around
dropping crisp packets like you do
where would we be?'

(Anthony didn't know, so she told him)

'We'd be wading waist-high in crisp packets,
that's where!'

Anthony was silent.
He hung his head.

It looked to the teacher
as if he was very sorry.

When in fact he was trying to calculate
just how many packets it would take
to bring Basildon to a complete standstill.

LINDSAY MacRAE

CHILDREN

If children live with criticism
   they learn to condemn

If children live with hostility
   they learn to fight

If children live with ridicule
   they learn to be shy

If children live with shame
   they learn to feel guilty

If children live with tolerance
   they learn to be patient

If children live with encouragement
   they learn confidence

If children live with praise
   they learn to appreciate

If children live with fairness
   they learn justice

If children live with security
   they learn to have faith

If children live with approval
   they learn to like themselves

If children live with acceptance and friendship
   they learn to find love in the world

ANONYMOUS

LITTLE ORPHANT ANNIE

Little Orphant Annie's come to our house to stay,
An' wash the cups an' saucers up, an' brush the crumbs away,
An' shoo the chickens off the porch, an' dust the hearth an' sweep,
An' make the fire, an' bake the bread, an' earn her board-an'-keep;
An' all us other childern, when the supper things is done,
We set around the kitchen fire an' has the mostest fun
A-list'nin' to the witch-tales 'at Annie tells about,
An' the Gobble-uns 'at gits you
   Ef you
      Don't
         Watch
            Out!

Onc't they was a little boy wouldn't say his prayers, –
So when he went to bed at night, away up stairs,
His Mammy heerd him holler, an' his Daddy heerd him bawl,
An' when they turn't the kivvers down, he wasn't there at all!
An' they seeked him in the rafter-room, an' cubby-hole, an' press,
An' seeked him up the chimbly-flue, an' ever'wheres, I guess;
But all they ever found was thist his pants an' roundabout –
An' the Gobble-uns'll git you
    Ef you
      Don't
        Watch
          Out!

An' one time a little girl 'ud allus laugh an' grin,
An' make fun of ever'one, an' all her blood an' kin;
An' onc't, when they was 'company', an' ole folks was there,
She mocked 'em an' shocked 'em, an' said she didn't care!
An' thist as she kicked her heels, an' turn't to run an' hide,
They was two great big Black Things a-standin' by her side,
An' they snatched her through the ceilin' 'fore she knowed what
   she's about!
An' the Gobble-uns'll git you
    Ef you
      Don't
        Watch
          Out!

An' little Orphant Annie says when the blaze is blue,
An' the lamp-wick sputters, an' the wind goes woo-oo!
An' you hear the crickets quit, an' the moon is grey,
An' the lightnin'-bugs in dew is all squenched away, –

You better mind yer parents, an' yer teachers fond an' dear,
An' churish them 'at loves you, an' dry the orphant tear,
An he'p the pore an' needy ones 'at clusters all about,
Er the Gobble-uns'll git you
   Ef you
      Don't
         Watch
            Out!

JAMES WHITCOMB RILEY

FIREWORK NIGHT

The sky is filled with sparks and flames;
the children rush about,
their cries are hardly heard among
the din of bangers, jumping jacks and rockets.

Dogs howl and cats cry –
Frightened of the noise.
The sky is filled with cordite smoke.
The fire is burning high.
Flashes here and crackles there.
A rocket soars into the sky.

Among all this noise nobody hears
a small child sobbing in the shade,
a banger exploded in his hand
and only he can feel the pain.

ERIC SIMPSON

CONVERSATION PIECE

Late again Blenkinsop?
What's the excuse this time?
Not my fault sir.
Whose fault is it then?
Grandma's sir.
Grandma's. What did she do?
She died sir.
Died?
She's seriously dead all right sir.
That makes four grandmothers this term.
And all on P.E. days Blenkinsop.
I know. It's very upsetting sir.
How many grandmothers have you got Blenkinsop?
Grandmothers sir? None sir.
None?
All dead sir.
And what about yesterday Blenkinsop?
What about yesterday sir?
You missed maths.
That was the dentist sir.
The dentist died?
No sir. My teeth sir.
You missed the test Blenkinsop.
I'd been looking forward to it too sir.
Right, line up for P.E.
Can't sir.
No such word as can't. Why can't you?
No kit sir.
Where is it?

Home sir.
What's it doing at home?
Not ironed sir.
Couldn't you iron it?
Can't do it sir.
Why not?
My hand sir.
Who usually does it?
Grandma sir.
Why couldn't she do it?
Dead sir.

GARETH OWEN

EILY KILBRIDE

On the north side of Cork city
Where I sported and played
On the banks of my own lovely Lee
Having seen the goat break loose in Grand Parade

I met a child, Eily Kilbride
Who'd never heard of marmalade,
Whose experience of breakfast
Was coldly limited,

Whose entire school day
Was a bag of crisps,
Whose parents had no work to do,

Who went, once, into the countryside,
Saw a horse with a feeding bag over its head
And thought it was sniffing glue.

BRENDAN KENNELLY

BOY AT THE WINDOW

Seeing the snowman standing all alone
In dusk and cold is more than he can bear.
The small boy weeps to hear the wind prepare
A night of gnashings and enormous moan.
His tearful sight can hardly reach to where
The pale-faced figure with bitumen eyes
Returns him such a god-forsaken stare
As outcast Adam gave to Paradise.

The man of snow is, nonetheless, content,
Having no wish to go inside and die.
Still, he is moved to see the youngster cry.
Though frozen water is his element,
He melts enough to drop from one soft eye
A trickle of the purest rain, a tear
For the child at the bright pane surrounded by
Such warmth, such light, such love, and so much fear.

RICHARD WILBUR

EXPERIMENT

at school we're doing growing things
  with cress.
sprinkly seeds in plastic pots
  of cotton wool.

Kate's cress sits up on the sill
  she gives it water.
mine is shut inside the cupboard
  dark and dry.

now her pot has great big clumps
  of green
mine hasn't.
Mrs Martin calls it Science
  I call it mean.

DANIELLE SENSIER

IN MRS TILSCHER'S CLASS

You could travel up the Blue Nile
with your finger, tracing the route
while Mrs Tilscher chanted the scenery.
Tana. Ethiopia. Khartoum. Aswan.
That for an hour, then a skittle of milk
and the chalky Pyramids rubbed into dust.
A window opened with a long pole.
The laugh of a bell swung by a running child.

This was better than home. Enthralling books.
The classroom glowed like a sweet shop.
Sugar paper. Coloured shapes. Brady and Hindley
faded, like the faint, uneasy smudge of a mistake.
Mrs Tilscher loved you. Some mornings, you found
she'd left a good gold star by your name.
The scent of a pencil slowly, carefully, shaved.
A xylophone's nonsense heard from another form.

Over the Easter term, the inky tadpoles changed
from commas into exclamation marks. Three frogs
hopped in the playground, freed by a dunce,
followed by a line of kids, jumping and croaking
away from the lunch queue. A rough boy
told you how you were born. You kicked him, but stared
at your parents, appalled, when you got back home.

That feverish July, the air tasted of electricity.
A tangible alarm made you always untidy, hot,
fractious under the heavy, sexy sky. You asked her
how you were born and Mrs Tilscher smiled,
then turned away. Reports were handed out.
You ran through the gates, impatient to be grown,
as the sky split open into a thunderstorm.

CAROL ANN DUFFY

THE APPLE-RAID

Darkness came early, though not yet cold;
Stars were strung on the telegraph wires;
Street lamps spilled pools of liquid gold;
The breeze was spiced with garden fires.

That smell of burnt leaves, the early dark,
Can still excite me but not as it did
So long ago when we met in the park –
Myself, John Peters and David Kidd.

We moved out of town to the district where
The lucky and wealthy had their homes
With garages, gardens, and apples to spare
Clustered in the trees' green domes.

We chose the place we meant to plunder
And climbed the wall and tip-toed through
The secret dark. Apples crunched under
Our feet as we moved through the grass and dew.

We found the lower boughs of a tree
That were easy to reach. We stored the fruit
In pockets and jerseys until all three
Boys were heavy with their tasty loot.

Safe on the other side of the wall
We moved back to town and munched as we went.
I wonder if David remembers at all
That little adventure, the apples' fresh scent.

Strange to think that he's fifty years old,
That tough little boy with scabs on his knees;
Stranger to think that John Peters lies cold
In an orchard in France beneath apple trees.

VERNON SCANNELL

EXPERIMENTS

I was not unhappy
At school, made something
Of the lessons over the gold heads
Of the girls. Love, said
The letters on
The blackboard. Love, I wrote down
In my book.
       There was one room,
However, that was full of
Jars, test-tubes
And wet sinks. Poisonous smells
Came from it, rumours,
Reports. The pupils who
Worked there had glasses and
Tall skulls. They were pale and
Looked at us as though we were part
Of a boring experiment.

R.S. THOMAS

FROM FATHER TO SON

There is no limit to the number of times
Your father can come to life, and he is as tender as ever
    he was
And as poor, his overcoat buttoned to the throat,
His face blue from the wind that always blows in the outer
    darkness
He comes toward you, hesitant,
Unwilling to intrude and yet driven at the point of love
To this encounter.

You may think
That love is all that is left of him, but when he comes
He comes with all his winters and all his wounds.
He stands shivering in the empty street,
Cold and worn like a tramp at the end of a journey
And yet a shape of unquestioning love that you
Uneasy and hesitant of the cold touch of death
Must embrace.

Then, before you can touch him
He is gone, leaving on your fingers
A little more of his weariness
A little more of his love.

EMYR HUMPHREYS

BORED WORK

Our teacher on the blackboard writes twelve words
and dusty silence settles on us yobs
who have to fit them into sentences
so we can learn and so get proper jobs.

He's all over the place that diligent.
He wrote down twelve but it was tenement.

There once was a squatter in persistent.
The nomad a pointed hat on his head.
I shoved minute in his sleeping bag.
'I can't stand distinct in here,' he said.

I get a potato clock.
Idolize in bed till noon.
Does that mean about meander
That she'll dilate and I'll die soon.

Hands that judicious can be soft as your face.
It's really no wonder I'm sick of displace.

BARRIE WADE

PLAYGROUNDS

Playgrounds are such gobby places.
Know what I mean?
Everyone seems to have something to
Talk about, giggle, whisper, scream and shout about,
I mean, it's like being in a parrot cage.

And playgrounds are such pushy places.
Know what I mean?
Everyone seems to have to
Run about, jump, kick, do cartwheels, handstands, fly around,
I mean, it's like being inside a whirlwind.

And playgrounds are such patchy places.
Know what I mean?
Everyone seems to
Go round in circles, lines and triangles, coloured shapes,
I mean, it's like being in a kaleidoscope.

And playgrounds are such pally places.
Know what I mean?
Everyone seems to
Have best friends, secrets, link arms, be in gangs.
Everyone, except me.

Know what I mean?

BERLIE DOHERTY

MISS! SUE IS KISSING

Miss! Sue is kissing
the tadpoles again.
She is, Miss. I did,
I asked her. She said
something about catching
him young. Getting one
her own age. I don't know,
Miss. She keeps whispering
'Prince, Prince.' Isn't that
a dog's name, Miss?

MICHAEL HARRISON

TO A CHILD DANCING IN THE WIND

Dance there upon the shore;
What need have you to care
For wind or water's roar?
And tumble out your hair
That the salt drops have wet;
Being young you have not known
The fool's triumph, nor yet
Love lost as soon as won,
Nor the best labourer dead
And all the sheaves to bind.
What need have you to dread
The monstrous crying of wind?

W. B. YEATS

IN SCHOOL-DAYS

Still sits the school-house by the road,
    A ragged beggar sleeping;
Around it still the sumachs grow,
    And blackberry vines are creeping.

Within, the master's desk is seen,
    Deep scarred by raps official;
The warping floor, the battered seats,
    The jack-knife's carved initial;

The charcoal frescoes on its wall;
    Its door's worn sill, betraying
The feet that, creeping slow to school,
    Went storming out to playing!

Long years ago a winter sun
    Shone over it at setting;
Lit up its western window-panes,
    And low eaves' icy fretting.

It touched the tangled golden curls,
    And brown eyes full of grieving,
Of one who still her steps delayed
    When all the school were leaving.

For near her stood the little boy
    Her childish favour singled:
His cap pulled low upon a face
    Where pride and shame were mingled.

Pushing with restless feet the snow
    To right and left, he lingered –
As restlessly her tiny hands
    The blue-checked apron fingered.

He saw her lift her eyes; he felt
    The soft hand's light caressing,
And heard the tremble of her voice,
    As if a fault confessing.

'I'm sorry that I spelt the word:
    I hate to go above you,
Because' – the brown eyes lower fell –
    'Because, you see, I love you!'

Still memory to a grey-haired man
    That sweet child-face is showing.
Dear girl! the grasses on her grave
    Have forty years been growing.

He lives to learn, in life's hard school,
    How few who pass above him
Lament their triumph and his loss,
    Like her, – because they love him.

JOHN GREENLEAF WHITTIER

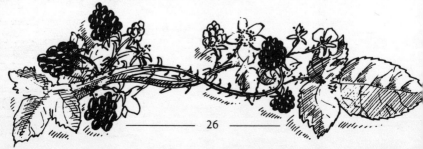

MOTHER TO SON

Well, son, I'll tell you:
Life for me ain't been no crystal stair.
It's had tacks in it,
And splinters,
And boards torn up,
And places with no carpet on the floor –
Bare.
But all the time
I'se been a-climbin' on,
And reachin' landin's,
And turnin' corners,
And sometimes goin' in the dark
Where there ain't been no light.
So, boy, don't you turn back.
Don't you set down on the steps
'Cause you find it kinder hard.
Don't you fall now –
For I'se still goin', honey,
I'se still climbin',
And life for me ain't been no crystal stair.

LANGSTON HUGHES

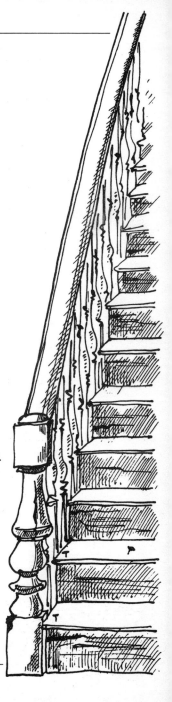

27

TOO MANY DAVES

Did I ever tell you that Mrs McCave
Had twenty-three sons and she named them all Dave?
Well, she did. And that wasn't a smart thing to do.
You see, when she wants one and calls out, 'Yoo-Hoo!
Come into the house, Dave!' she doesn't get one.
All twenty-three Daves of hers come on the run!
This makes things quite difficult at the McCaves'
As you can imagine, with so many Daves.
And often she wishes that, when they were born,
She had named one of them Bodkin Van Horn
And one of them Hoos-Foos. And one of them Snimm.
And one of them Hot-Shot. And one Sunny Jim.
And one of them Shadrack. And one of them Blinkey.
And one of them Stuffy. And one of them Stinkey.
Another one Putt-Putt. Another one Moon Face.
Another one Marvin O'Gravel Balloon Face.
And one of them Ziggy. And one Soggy Muff.
One Buffalo Bill. And one Biffalo Buff.
And one of them Sneepy. And one Weepy Weed.
And one Paris Garters. And one Harris Tweed.
And one of them Sir Michael Carmichael Zutt
And one of them Oliver Boliver Butt
And one of them Zanzibar Buck-Buck McFate ...
But she didn't do it. And now it's too late.

DR SEUSS (THEODORE GEISEL)

HEARING THAT HIS FRIEND WAS COMING BACK FROM THE WAR

In old days those who went to fight
In three years had one year's leave.
But in this war the soldiers are never changed;
They must go on fighting till they die
  on the battlefield.
I thought of you, so weak and indolent,
Hopelessly trying to learn to march and drill.
That a young man should ever come home again
Seemed about as likely as that the sky should fall.
Since I got the news that you were coming back,
Twice I have mounted to the high wall of your home.
I found your brother mending your horse's stall;
I found your mother sewing your new clothes.
I am half afraid; perhaps it is not true;
Yet I never weary of watching for you on the road.
Each day I go out at the City Gate
With a flask of wine, lest you should come thirsty.
Oh that I could shrink the surface of the World,
So that suddenly I might find you standing at my side!

WANG CHIEN

UNCLE EDWARD'S AFFLICTION

Uncle Edward was colour-blind;
We grew accustomed to the fact.
When he asked someone to hand him
The green book from the window-seat
And we observed its bright red cover
Either apathy or tact
Stifled comment. We passed it over.
Much later, I began to wonder
What curious world he wandered in,
Down streets where pea-green pillar-boxes
Grinned at a fire-engine as green;
How Uncle Edward's sky at dawn
And sunset flooded marshy green.
Did he ken John Peel with his coat so green
And Robin Hood in Lincoln Red?
On country walks avoid being stung
By nettles hot as a witch's tongue?
What meals he savoured with his eyes:
Green strawberries and fresh red peas,
Green beef and greener burgundy.
All unscientific, so it seems:
His world was not at all like that,
So those who claim to know have said.
Yet, I believe, in war-smashed France
He must have crawled from neutral mud
To lie in pastures dark and red
And seen, appalled, on every blade
The rain of innocent green blood.

VERNON SCANNELL

THE NIGHT BEFORE LARRY WAS STRETCHED

The night before Larry was stretched,
The boys they all paid him a visit;
A bait in their sacks too they fetched,
They sweated their duds till they riz it;
For Larry was always the lad,
When a friend was condemned to the squeezer,
Would fence all the togs that he had
Just to help the poor boy to a sneezer,
And moisten his gob 'fore he died.

The boys they came crowding in fast,
They drew all their stools round about him,
Six glims round his trap-case they placed;
He couldn't be well waked without 'em.
I axed was he fit for to die
Without having truly repented?
Says Larry, 'That's all in my eye,
And first by the clergy invented,
To get a fat bit for themselves.'

'I'm sorry now, Larry,' says I,
'to see you in this situation;
And, blister my limbs if I lie,
I'd as lief it had been my own station.'
'Och hone! 'tis all over,' says he,
'For the neck-cloth I'll be forced to put on,
And by this time tomorrow you'll see
Your Larry will be dead as mutton,
Because why, his courage was good.

'And I'll be cut up like a pie,
And my knob from my body be parted.'
'You're in the wrong box then,' says I,
'For blast me if they're so hard-hearted;
A chalk on the back of your neck
Is all that Jack Ketch dares to give you;
Then mind not such trifles a feck,
For why should the likes of them grieve you?
And now boys, come tip us the deck.'
The cards being called for, they played,
Till Larry found one of them cheated;
A dart at his napper he made
(The boy being easily heated);
'Oh! by the hokey, you thief,
I'll scuttle your knob with my daddle!
You cheat me because I'm in grief,
But soon I'll demolish your noddle,
And leave you your claret to drink.'

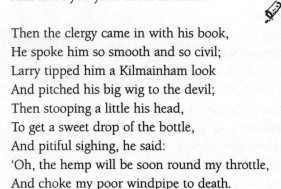

Then the clergy came in with his book,
He spoke him so smooth and so civil;
Larry tipped him a Kilmainham look
And pitched his big wig to the devil;
Then stooping a little his head,
To get a sweet drop of the bottle,
And pitiful sighing, he said:
'Oh, the hemp will be soon round my throttle,
And choke my poor windpipe to death.

'Though sure it's the best way to die,
Oh! the devil a better a-living'!
For when the gallows is high,
Your journey is shorter to heaven.'
But what harasses Larry the most,
And makes his poor soul melancholy,
Is he thinks of the time when his ghost
Will come in a sheet to sweet Molly;
'Oh, sure it will kill her alive!'

So moving these last words he spoke,
We all vented our tears in a shower;
For my part I thought my heart broke,
To see him cut down like a flower.
On his travels we watched him next day;
Oh, the throttler, I thought I could kill him;
But Larry not one word did say,
Nor changed till he came to King William,
Then musha, his colour turned white.

When he came to the nubbing chit,
He was tucked up so neat and so pretty;
The rumbler jogged off from his feet,
And he died with his face to the city;
He kicked too, but that was all pride,
For soon you might see 'twas all over;
Soon after, the noose was untied,
And at darkee we waked him in clover,
And sent him to take a ground sweat.

ANONYMOUS

THE CHOOSING

We were first equal Mary and I
with the same coloured ribbons in mouse-coloured hair,
and with equal shyness
we curtseyed to the lady councillor
for copies of Collins' Children's Classics.
First equal, equally proud.

Best friends too Mary and I
a common bond in being cleverest (equal)
in our small school's small class.
I remember
the competition for top desk
or to read aloud the lesson
at school service.
And my terrible fear
of her superiority at sums.

I remember the housing scheme
Where we both stayed.
The same house, different homes,
where the choices were made.

I don't know exactly why they moved,
but anyway they went.
Something about a three-apartment
and a cheaper rent.
But from the top deck of the high-school bus
I'd glimpse among the others on the corner
Mary's father, mufflered, contrasting strangely
with the elegant greyhounds by his side.

He didn't believe in high-school education,
especially for girls,
or in forking out for uniforms.

Ten years later on a Saturday –
I am coming home from the library –
sitting near me on the bus,
Mary
with a husband who is tall,
curly haired, has eyes
for no one else but Mary.
Her arms are round the full-shaped vase
that is her body.
Oh, you can see where the attraction lies
in Mary's life –
not that I envy her, really.

And I am coming from the library
with my arms full of books.
I think of the prizes that were ours for the taking
and wonder when the choices got made
we don't remember making.

LIZ LOCHHEAD

ANOREXIC

My father's sister,
the one who died
before there was a word for it,
was fussy with her food.
'Eat up,' they'd say to me,
ladling a bowl with warning.

What I remember's
how she'd send me to the dairy,
taught me to take cream,
the standing gold.
Where the jug dipped
I saw its blue-milk skin
before the surface healed.

Breath held, tongue between teeth,
I carried in the cream,
brimmed, level,
parallel, I knew,
with that other, hidden horizon
of the earth's deep
ungleaming water-table.

And she, more often than not half-dressed,
stockings, a slip, a Chinese kimono,
would warm that cream, pour it
with crumbled melting cheese
over a delicate white cauliflower,
or field mushrooms
steaming in porcelain,

then watch us eat, relishing,
smoking her umpteenth cigarette,
glamorous, perfumed, starved,
and going to die.

GILLIAN CLARKE

WATER EVERYWHERE

There's water on the ceiling,
And water on the wall,
There's water in the bedroom,
And water in the hall,
There's water on the landing,
And water on the stair,
Whenever Daddy takes a bath
There's water everywhere.

VALERIE BLOOM

DAD

Your old hat hurts me, and those black
  fat raisins you liked to press into
my palm from your soft heavy hand:
  I see you staggering back up the path
with sacks of potatoes from some local farm,
  fresh eggs, flowers. Every day I grieve

for your great heart broken and you gone.
  You loved to watch the trees. This year
you did not see their Spring.
  The sky was freezing over the fen
as on that somewhere secretly appointed day
  you beached: cold, white-faced, shivering.

What happened, old bull, my loyal
  hoarse-voiced warrior? The hammer
blow that stopped you in your track
  and brought you to a hospital monitor
could not destroy your courage
  to the end you were
uncowed and unconcerned with pleasing anyone.

I think of you now as once again safely
  at my mother's side, the earth as
chosen as a bed, and feel most sorrow for
  all that was gentle in
my childhood buried there
  already forfeit, now forever lost.

ELAINE FEINSTEIN

THE LAST WORDS OF MY ENGLISH GRANDMOTHER

There were some dirty plates
and a glass of milk
beside her on a small table
near the rank, dishevelled bed –

Wrinkled and nearly blind
she lay and snored
rousing with anger in her tones
to cry for food,

Gimme something to eat –
They're starving me –
I'm all right I won't go
to the hospital. No, no, no

Give me something to eat
Let me take you
to the hospital, I said
and after you are well

you can do as you please.
She smiled, Yes
you do what you please first
then I can do what I please –

Oh, oh, oh! she cried
as the ambulance men lifted
her to the stretcher –
Is that what you call

making me comfortable?
By now her mind was clear –
Oh you think you're smart
you young people,

she said, but I'll tell you
you don't know anything.
Then we started.
On the way

we passed a long row
of elms. She looked at them
awhile out of
the ambulance window and said,

What are all those
fuzzy looking things out there?
Trees? Well, I'm tired
of them, and rolled her head away.

WILLIAM CARLOS WILLIAMS

THE LIGHT OF OTHER DAYS

Oft, in the stilly night,
  Ere slumber's chain has bound me,
Fond Memory brings the light
  Of other days around me:
    The smiles, the tears
    Of boyhood's years,
  The words of love then spoken;
    The eyes that shone,
    Now dimmed and gone,
  The cheerful hearts now broken!
Thus, in the stilly night,
  Ere slumber's chain has bound me,
Sad Memory brings the light
  Of other days around me.

When I remember all
  The friends, so linked together,
I've seen around me fall
  Like leaves in wintry weather,
    I feel like one
    Who treads alone
  Some banquet-hall deserted,
    Whose lights are fled,
    Whose garlands dead,
  And all but he departed!
Thus, in the stilly night,
  Ere slumber's chain has bound me,
Sad Memory brings the light
  Of other days around me.

THOMAS MOORE

HOLIDAYS AT HOME

There was a family who, every year,
Would go abroad, sometimes to Italy,
Sometimes to France. The youngest did not dare
To say, 'I much prefer to stay right here.'

You see, abroad there were no slot-machines,
No bright pink rock with one name going through it,
No rain, no boarding-houses, no baked beans,
No landladies, and no familiar scenes.

And George, the youngest boy, so longed to say,
'I don't like Greece, I don't like all these views,
I don't like having fierce sun every day,
And, most of all, I just detest the way

The food is cooked – that garlic and that soup,
Those strings of pasta, and no cakes at all.'
The family wondered why George seemed to droop
And looked just like a thin hen in a coop.

They never guessed why when they said, 'Next year
We can't afford abroad, we'll stay right here,'
George looked so pleased and soon began to dream
Of piers, pink rock, deep sand, and Devonshire cream.

ELIZABETH JENNINGS

OLD SMOOTHING IRON

Often I watched her lift it
from where its compact wedge
rode the back of the stove
like a tug at anchor.

To test its heat she'd stare
and spit in its iron face
or hold it up next her cheek
to divine the stored danger.

Soft thumps on the ironing board.
Her dimpled angled elbow
and intent stoop
as she aimed the smoothing iron

like a plane into linen,
like the resentment of women.
To work, her dumb lunge says,
is to move a certain mass

through a certain distance,
is to pull your weight and feel
exact and equal to it.
Feel dragged upon. And buoyant.

SEAMUS HEANEY

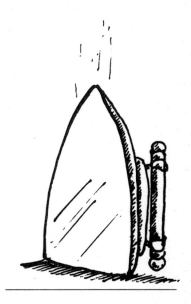

43

ON PRINCE FREDERICK

Here lies Fred,
Who was alive and is dead:
Had it been his father,
I had much rather;
Had it been his brother
Still better than another;
Had it been his sister,
No one would have missed her;
Had it been the whole generation,
So much the better for the nation:
But since 'tis only Fred,
Who was alive and is dead,
There's no more to be said.

ANONYMOUS

A NUN TAKES THE VEIL

That morning early I ran through briars
To catch the calves that were bound for market.
I stopped the once, to watch the sun
Rising over Doolin across the water.

The calves were tethered outside the house
While I had my breakfast: the last one at home
For forty years. I had what I wanted (they said
I could), so we'd loaf bread and Marie biscuits.

We strung the calves behind the boat,
Me keeping clear to protect my style:
Confirmation suit and my patent sandals.
But I trailed my fingers in the cool green water,

Watching the puffins driving homeward
To their nests on Aran. On the Galway mainland
I tiptoed clear of the cow-dunged slipway
And watched my brothers heaving the calves

As they lost their footing. We went in a trap,
Myself and my mother, and I said goodbye
To my father then. The last I saw of him
Was a hat and jacket and a salley stick,

Driving cattle to Ballyvaughan.
He died (they told me) in the county home,
Asking to see me. But that was later:
As we trotted on through the morning mist,

I saw a car for the first time ever,
Hardly seeing it before it vanished.
I couldn't believe it, and I stood up looking
To where I could hear its noise departing

But it was only a glimpse. That night in the convent
The sisters spoilt me, but I couldn't forget
The morning's vision, and I fell asleep
With the engine humming through the open window.

BERNARD O'DONOGHUE

UH-OH
(The last words spoken by the captain of the spaceship Challenger)

uh-oh
he said

they were
at
the pinnacle
of human
achievement

they wore
white space-suits

he had talked
to
the president
on the
telephone
the day before

little boys
played with models
of their
spaceship

they were headed
straight up

he had kissed
his girl-friend
the night before

tired his mind
on other things

she touched
his tense muscles

'it's just a job
to those guys'

his mother couldn't
think of what
to give him

settled on
home-made jam
for his wife

it was a life
he hadn't
really chosen

he had just
over-achieved

what had the
president
said?

his wife asked

oh, i don't know

it wasn't like
they were going
to the moon

that had been
done already

good luck, i suppose

good luck
yes
that was probably it

that was probably
what the president
had said

words to that effect

and now the little
meter
had gone red
all of a sudden
and there was
nothing he could do

no split-second
decision

taken out
of his hands

just a little
surprised

that the routine
should be
interruped
like that

OLIVER DUNNE

ROMANCE

When I was but thirteen or so
  I went into a golden land,
Chimborazo, Cotopaxi
  Took me by the hand.

My father died, my brother too.
  They passed like fleeting dreams.
I stood where Popocatapetl
  In the sunlight gleams.

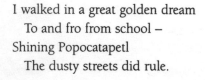

I dimly heard the Master's voice
  And boys far-off at play,
Chimborazo, Cotopaxi
  Had stolen me away.

I walked in a great golden dream
  To and fro from school –
Shining Popocatapetl
  The dusty streets did rule.

I walked home with a gold dark boy
  And never a word I'd say,
Chimborazo, Cotopaxi
  Had taken my speech away:

I gazed entranced upon his face
  Fairer than any flower –
O shining Popocatapetl
  It was thy magic hour:

The houses, people, traffic seemed
　　Thin fading dreams by day,
Chimborazo, Cotopaxi
　　They had stolen my soul away!

WALTER JAMES TURNER

THERE WAS AN INDIAN

There was an Indian, who had known no change,
Who strayed content along a sunlit beach
Gathering shells. He heard a sudden strange
Commingled noise; looked up; and gasped for speech.
For in the bay, where nothing was before,
Moved on the sea, by magic, huge canoes,
With bellying cloths on poles, and not one oar,
And fluttering coloured signs and clambering crews.
And he, in fear, this naked man alone,
His fallen hands forgetting all their shells,
His lips gone pale, knelt low behind a stone,
And stared, and saw, and did not understand,
Columbus's doom-burdened caravels
Slant to the shore, and all their seamen land.

SIR JOHN SQUIRE

THE HORSE THAT HAD A FLAT TYRE

Once upon a valley
there came down
from some goldenblue mountains
a handsome young prince
who was riding
a dawncoloured horse
named Lordsburg.

> I love you
> You're my breathing castle
> Gentle so gentle
> We'll live forever

In the valley
there was a beautiful maiden
whom the prince
drifted into love with
like a New Mexico made from
apple thunder and long
glass beads.

> I love you
> You're my breathing castle
> Gentle so gentle
> We'll live forever

The prince enchanted
the maiden
and they rode off
on the dawncoloured horse
named Lordsburg
toward the goldenblue mountains.

I love you
You're my breathing castle
Gentle so gentle
We'll live forever

They would have lived
happily ever after
if the horse hadn't had
a flat tyre
in front of a dragon's
house.

RICHARD BRAUTIGAN

THE RESCUE

The boy climbed up into the tree.
The tree rocked; so did he.
He was trying to rescue a cat,
A cushion of a cat, from where it sat
In a high crutch of branches, mewing
As though to say to him, 'Nothing doing,'

Whenever he shouted, 'Come on, come down.'
So up he climbed, and the whole town
Lay at his feet, round him the leaves
Fluttered like a lady's sleeves,
And the cat sat, and the wind blew so
That he would have flown had he let go.
At last he was high enough to scoop
That fat white cushion or nincompoop
And tuck her under his arm, and turn
To go down –
       But oh! he began to learn
How high he was, how hard it would be
Having come up with four limbs, to go down with three.
His heart-beats knocked as he tried to think:
He would put the cat in a lower chink –
She appealed to him with a cry of alarm
And put her eighteen claws in his arm.
So he stayed looking down for a minute or so
To the good ground so far below.
When the minute started he saw it was hard;
When it ended he couldn't move a yard.

So there he was stuck, in the failing light

And the wind rising with the coming of the night.
His father! He shouted for all he was worth.
His father came nearer: 'What on earth – ?'
'I've got the cat up here but I'm stuck.'
'Hold on .... ladder ...', he heard. Oh, luck!
How lovely behind the branches tossing
The globes at the pedestrian crossing
And the big fluorescent lamps glowed
Mauve-green on the main road.
But his father didn't come back, didn't come;
His little fingers were going numb.

The cat licked them as though to say
'Are you feeling cold? I'm OK.'
He wanted to cry, he would count ten first,
But just as he was ready to burst,
A torch came and his father and mother
And a ladder and the dog and his younger brother.
Up on a big branch stood his father,
His mother came to the top of the ladder,
His brother stood on a lower rung,
The dog sat still and put out its tongue.
From one to another the cat was handed
And afterwards she was reprimanded.
After that it was easy, though the wind blew:
The parents came down, the boy came too
From the ladder, the lower branch and the upper
And all of them went indoors to supper,
And the tree rocked and the moon sat
In the branches like a white cat.

HAL SUMMERS

BISHOP HATTO

The summer and autumn had been so wet
That in winter the corn was growing yet;
'Twas a piteous sight to see all around
The grain lie rotting on the ground.

Every day the starving poor
Crowded around Bishop Hatto's door,
For he had a plentiful last-year's store,
And all the neighbourhood could tell
His granaries were furnish'd well.

At last Bishop Hatto appointed a day
To quiet the poor without delay;
He bade them to his great barn repair,
And they should have food for the winter there.

Rejoiced such tidings good to hear,
The poor folk flock'd from far and near;
The great barn was full as it could hold
Of women and children, and young and old.

Then when he saw it could hold no more,
Bishop Hatto he made fast the door,
And while for mercy on Christ they call,
He set fire to the barn and burnt them all.

'I' faith, 'tis an excellent bonfire!' quoth he,
'And the country is greatly obliged to me,
For ridding it in these times forlorn
Of rats, that only consume the corn.'

So then to his palace returned he,
And he sat down to supper merrily,
And he slept that night like an innocent man.
But Bishop Hatto never slept again.

In the morning as he enter'd the hall,
Where his pictures hung against the wall,
A sweat like death all over him came;
For the rats had eaten it out of the frame.

As he look'd there came a man from his farm,
He had a countenance white with alarm;
'My lord, I open'd your granaries this morn,
And the rats had eaten all your corn.'

Another came running presently,
And he was pale as pale could be;
'Fly! my Lord Bishop, fly!' quoth he,
'Ten thousand rats are coming this way –
The Lord forgive you for yesterday!'

Bishop Hatto fearfully hasten'd away,
And he crossed the Rhine without delay,
And reach'd his tower, and barr'd with care
All the windows, doors, and loopholes there.

He laid him down and closed his eyes,
But soon a scream made him arise;
He started, and saw two eyes of flame
On his pillows from whence the screaming came.

He listen'd and look'd; it was only the cat;
But the Bishop grew more fearful for that,
For she sat screaming, mad with fear,
At the army of rats that was drawing near.

For they have swum over the river so deep,
And they have climb'd the shores so steep,
And up the tower their way is bent,
To do the work for which they were sent.

They are not to be told by the dozen or score;
By thousands they come, and by myriads and more;
Such numbers had never been heard of before,
Such a judgement had never been witness'd of yore.

Down on his knees the Bishop fell,
And faster and faster his beads did he tell,
As louder and louder drawing near
The gnawing of their teeth he could hear.

And in at the windows, and in at the door,
And through the walls helter-skelter they pour,
And down from the ceiling, and up through the floor,
From the right and left, from behind and before,
From within and without, from above and below,
And all at once to the Bishop they go.

They have whetted their teeth against the stones,
And now they pick the Bishop's bones;
They gnaw'd the flesh from every limb,
For they were sent to do judgement on him!

ROBERT SOUTHEY

THE MISTLETOE BOUGH

The mistletoe hung in the castle hall,
The holly branch shone on the old oak wall;
And the baron's retainers were blithe and gay,
And keeping their Christmas holiday.
The baron beheld with a father's pride
His beautiful child, young Lovell's bride;
While she with her bright eyes seem'd to be
The star of the goodly company.

'I'm weary of dancing now;' she cried;
'Here tarry a moment – I'll hide – I'll hide!
And, Lovell, be sure thou'rt first to trace
The clue to my secret lurking place.'
Away she ran – and her friends began
Each tower to search, and each nook to scan;
And young Lovell cried, 'Oh where dost thou hide?
I'm lonesome without thee, my own dear bride.'

They sought her that night! and they sought her next day!
And they sought her in vain when a week pass'd away!
In the highest – the lowest – the loneliest spot,
Young Lovell sought wildly – but found her not.
And years flew by, and their grief at last
Was told as a sorrowful tale long past;
And when Lovell appeared, the children cried,
'See! the old man weeps for his fairy bride.'

At length an oak chest, that had long lain hid,
Was found in the castle – they raised the lid –
And a skeleton form lay mouldering there,
In the bridal wreath of that lady fair!
Oh! sad was her fate! – in sportive jest
She hid from her lord in the old oak chest.
It closed with a spring! – and, dreadful doom,
The bride lay clasp'd in her living tomb!

THOMAS HAYNES BAYLY

GLANMORE SONNETS:
SONNET VII

Dogger, Rockall, Malin, Irish Sea:
Green, swift upsurges, North Atlantic flux
Conjured by that strong gale-warning voice
Collapse into a sibilant penumbra,
Midnight and closedown. Sirens of the tundra,
Of eel-road, seal-road, keel-road, whale-road, raise
Their wind-compounded keen behind the baize
And drive the trawlers to the lee of Wicklow.
L'Etoile, Le Guillemot, La Belle Hélène
Nursed their bright names this morning in the bay
That toiled like mortar. It was marvellous
And actual, I said out loud, 'A haven,'
The word deepening, clearing, like the sky
Elsewhere on Minches, Cromarty, The Faroes.

SEAMUS HEANEY

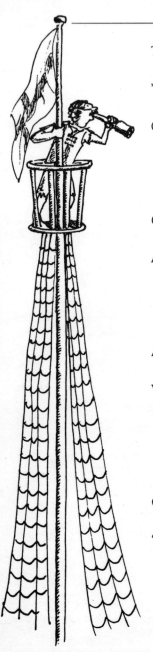

THE WHALE

'Twas in the year of forty-nine,
    On March, the twentieth day,
Our gallant ship her anchor weigh'd,
    And to the sea she bore away,
        Brave boys,
    And to the sea she bore away.

Old Blowhard was our captain's name,
    Our ship the Lion bold,
And we were bound to the North Country
    To face the frost and the cold.
        Brave boys,
    To face the frost and the cold.

And when we came to that cold country
    Where the ice and the snow do lie,
Where there's ice and snow, and the great
    whales blow,
    And the daylight does not die,
        Brave boys,
    And the daylight does not die.

Our mate went up to the topmast head
    With a spyglass in his hand:
'A whale, a whale, a whale,' he cries,
    'And she spouts at every span,'
        Brave boys,
    'And she spouts at every span.'

Up jumped old Blowhard on the deck –
   And a clever little man was he –
'Overhaul, overhaul, let your main-tackle fall,
   And launch your boat to sea,'
      Brave boys,
   'And launch your boat to sea.'

We struck that fish and away she flew
   With a flourish of her tail;
But oh! and alas! we lost one man
   And we did not catch that whale,
      Brave boys,
   And we did not catch that whale.

Now when the news to our captain came
   He called up all his crew,
And for the losing of that man
   He down his colours drew,
      Brave boys,
   He down his colours drew.

Says he: 'My men, be not dismayed
　　At the losing of one man,
For Providence will have his will,
　　Let man do what he can,'
　　　Brave boys,
　　Let man do what he can.

Now the losing of that prentice boy
　　It grieved our captain sore,
But the losing of that great big whale
　　It grieved him a damned sight more,
　　　Brave boys,
　　It grieved him a damned sight more.

TRADITIONAL

LORELEI

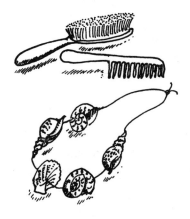

Lorelei, the story has it
You are sitting on some rocks,
And alluring and in-luring
Combing out your golden locks.

But the story misses out on
What you're really doing there;
You're assessing your reflection,
As you rearrange your hair.

And those suicides by water,
Though of course they gratify,
Whilst you wait for Captain Right, are
Mere fringe benefits, Lorelei.

GERDA MAYER

THE SURVIVORS

I never told you this.
He told me about it often:
Seven days in an open boat – burned out,
No time to get food:
Biscuits and water and the unwanted sun,
With only the oars' wing-beats for motion,
Labouring heavily towards land
That existed on a remembered chart,
Never on the horizon
Seven miles from the boat's bow.

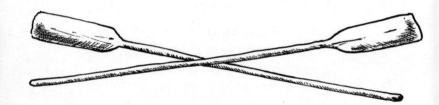

After two days song dried on their lips;
After four days speech.
On the fifth cracks began to appear
In the faces' masks; salt scorched them.
They began to think about death,
Each man to himself, feeding it
On what the rest could not conceal.
The sea was as empty as the sky,
A vast disc under a dome
Of the same vastness, perilously blue.

But on the sixth day towards evening
A bird passed. No one slept that night;
The boat had become an ear
Straining for the desired thunder
Of the wrecked waves. It was dawn when it came,
Ominous as the big guns
Of enemy shores. The men cheered it.
From the swell's rise one of them saw the ruins
Of all that sea, where a lean horseman
Rode towards them and with a rope
Galloped them up on to the curt sand.

R.S. THOMAS

From LAST VERSES

... Look, as your looking-glass by chance may fall,
Divide, and break in many pieces small
And yet shows forth the self-same face in all,

Proportions, features, graces, just the same,
And in the smallest piece as well the name
Of fairest one deserves as in the richest frame;

So all my thoughts are pieces but of you,
Which put together make a glass so true
As I therein no other's face but yours can view.

MICHAEL DRAYTON

THE HANGMAN'S TREE

'Hangman, hangman, hold your hand,
      O hold it just a while!
For there I see my father coming,
      Riding many a mile.

'Father, have you brought me gold?
      Will you set me free?
Or have you come to see me hung
      From the hangman's tree?'

'No, I haven't brought you gold,
      I will not set you free,
But I have come to see you hung
      From the hangman's tree.'

'Hangman, hangman, hold your hand,
      O hold it just a while!
For there I see my mother coming,
      Riding many a mile.

'Mother, have you brought me gold?
      Will you set me free?
Or have you come to see me hung
      From the hangman's tree?'

'No, I haven't brought you gold,
      I will not set you free,
But I have come to see you hung
      From the hangman's tree.'

'Hangman, hangman, hold your hand,
    O hold it just a while!
For there I see my sister coming,
    Riding many a mile.

'Sister, have you brought me gold?
    Will you set me free?
Or have you come to see me hung
    From the hangman's tree?'

'No, I haven't brought you gold,
    I will not set you free,
But I have come to see you hung
    From the hangman's tree.'

'Hangman, hangman, hold your hand,
    O hold it just a while!
For there I see my sweetheart coming,
    Riding many a mile.

'Sweetheart, have you brought me gold?
    Will you set me free?
Or have you come to see me hung
    From the hangman's tree?'

'Yes, O yes, I've brought you gold,
    I will set you free,
For I have come to take you down
    From the hangman's tree.'

TRADITIONAL

THE GARDENER

The gardener stood at the garden gate,
    A primrose in his hand;
He saw a lovely girl come by,
    Slim as a willow wand.

'O lady, can you fancy me,
    And will you share my life?
All my garden flowers are yours,
    If you will be my wife.

'The white lily will be your shirt
    It suits your body best;
With cornflowers in your hair,
    A red rose on your breast.

'Your gloves will be the marigold,
    Glittering on your hand;
Your dress will be the sweet-william
    That grows upon the bank.'

'Young man, I cannot be your wife;
    I fear it will not do.
Although you care for me,' she said,
    'I cannot care for you.

'As you've provided clothes for me
    Among the summer flowers,
So I'll provide some clothes for you
    Among the winter showers.

'The fallen snow will be your shirt,
    It suits your body best;
Your head will be wound with the eastern wind,
    With the cold rain on your breast.

'Your boots will be of the seaweed
    That drifts upon the tide;
Your horse will be the white wave –
    Leap on, young man, and ride!'

TRADITIONAL

WHITE IN THE MOON ...

White in the moon the long road lies,
  The moon stands blank above;
White in the moon the long road lies
  That leads me from my love.

Still hangs the hedge without a gust,
  Still, still the shadows stay:
My feet upon the moonlit dust
  Pursue the ceaseless way.

The world is round, so travellers tell,
  And straight though reach the track,
Trudge on, trudge on, 'twill all be well,
  The way will guide one back.

But ere the circle homeward hies
  Far, far must it remove:
White in the moon the long road lies
  That leads me from my love.

A.E. HOUSMAN

MY DRESS IS OLD

My dress is old, but at night the moon is kind.
Then I wear a beautiful moon-coloured dress.

Translated by *VIRGINIA DRIVING HAWK SNEVE*

LOVE AND AGE

I play'd with you 'mid cowslips blowing,
    When I was six and you were four;
When garlands weaving, flower-balls throwing,
    Were pleasures soon to please no more.
Through groves and meads, o'er grass and heather,
    With little playmates, to and fro,
We wander'd hand in hand together;
    But that was sixty years ago.

You grew a lovely roseate maiden,
    And still our early love was strong;
Still with no care our days were laden,
    They glided joyously along;
And I did love you very dearly,
    How dearly words want power to show;
I thought your heart was touch'd as nearly;
    But that was fifty years ago.
Then other lovers came around you,
    Your beauty grew from year to year,
And many a splendid circle found you
    The centre of its glittering sphere.
I saw you then, first vows forsaking,
    On rank and wealth your hand bestow;
O, then I thought my heart was breaking! –
    But that was forty years ago.

And I lived on, to wed another:
    No cause she gave me to repine;
And when I heard you were a mother,
    I did not wish the children mine.

My own young flock, in fair progression,
    Made up a pleasant Christmas row:
My joy in them was past expression;
    But that was thirty years ago.

You grew a matron plump and comely,
    You dwelt in fashion's brightest blaze;
My earthly lot was far more homely;
    But I too had my festal days.
No merrier eyes have ever glisten'd
    Around the hearth-stone's wintry glow,
Than when my youngest child was christen'd;
    But that was twenty years ago.

Time pass'd. My eldest girl was married,
    And I am now a grandsire grey;
One pet of four years old I've carried
    Among the wild-flower'd meads to play.
In our old fields of childish pleasure,
    Where now, as then, the cowslips blow,
She fills her basket's ample measure;
    And that is not ten years ago.

But though first love's impassion'd blindness
    Has pass'd away in colder light,
I still have thought of you with kindness,
    And shall do, till our last good-night.
The ever-rolling silent hours
    Will bring a time we shall not know,
When our young days of gathering flowers
    Will be an hundred years ago.

THOMAS LOVE PEACOCK

LA BELLE DAME SANS MERCI

O what can ail thee Knight at arms,
  Alone and palely loitering?
The sedge has withered from the Lake,
  And no birds sing!

O what can ail thee Knight at arms,
  So haggard, and so woe begone?
The Squirrel's granary is full
  And the harvest's done.

I see a lily on thy brow
  With anguish moist and fever dew,
And on thy cheeks a fading rose
  Fast withereth too.

I met a Lady in the meads
  Full beautiful, a faery's child,
Her hair was long, her foot was light,
  And her eyes were wild.

I made a Garland for her head,
  And bracelets too, and fragrant Zone;
She look'd at me as she did love
  And made sweet moan.

I set her on my pacing steed
  And nothing else saw all day long;
For sidelong would she bend and sing
  A faery's song.

She found me roots of relish sweet
  And honey wild and manna dew;
And sure in language strange she said –
  I love thee true.

She took me to her elfin grot,
  And there she wept and sigh'd full sore;
And there I shut her wild wild eyes
  With kisses four.

And there she lulled me asleep,
  And there I dream'd, Ah woe betide!
The latest dream I ever dreamt
  On the cold hill side.

I saw pale Kings, and Princes too,
  Pale warriors, death pale were they all;
They cried, 'La Belle Dame sans Merci
  Hath thee in thrall!'

I saw their starv'd lips in the gloam
  With horrid warning gaped wide,
And I awoke, and found me here
  On the cold hill's side.

And this is why I sojourn here
  Alone and palely loitering,
Though the sedge is withered from the Lake,
  And no birds sing.

JOHN KEATS

SONG

Sweetest love, I do not go
    For weariness of thee,
Nor in hope the world can show
    A fitter love for me;
      But since that I
Must die at last, 'tis best
To use myself in jest
    Thus by fain'd deaths to die.

Yesternight the sun went hence,
    And yet is here today,
He hath no desire nor sense,
    Nor half so short a way:
      Then fear not me,
But believe that I shall make
Speedier journeys, since I take
    More wings and spurs than he.

O how feeble is man's power,
    That if good fortune fall,
Cannot add another hour,
    Nor a lost hour recall!
      But come bad chance,
And we join to it our strength,
And we teach it art and length,
    Itself o'er us to advance.

When thou sigh'st, thou sigh'st not wind,
    But sigh'st my soul away,
When thou weep'st, unkindly kind,

My life's blood doth decay.
    It cannot be
That thou lov'st me, as thou say'st,
If in thine my life thou waste,
    Thou art the best of me.

Let not thy divining heart
    Forethink me any ill,
Destiny may take thy part,
    And may thy fears fulfil;
    But think that we
Are but turn'd aside to sleep;
They who one another keep
    Alive, ne'er parted be.

JOHN DONNE

APRIL RAIN SONG

Let the rain kiss you.
Let the rain beat upon your head with silver liquid drops.
Let the rain sing you a lullaby.

The rain makes still pools on the sidewalk.
The rain makes running pools in the gutter.
The rain plays a little sleep-song on our roof at night –

And I love the rain.

LANGSTON HUGHES

A RED, RED ROSE

O, my Luve's like a red, red rose,
  That's newly sprung in June.
O, my Luve's like the melodie
  That's sweetly play'd in tune.

As fair art thou, my bonnie lass,
  So deep in luve am I;
And I will love thee still, my dear,
  Till a' the seas gang dry.

Till a' the seas gang dry, my dear,
  And the rocks melt wi' the sun:
I will love thee still, my dear,
  While the sands o' life shall run:

And fare thee weel, my only luve!
  And fare thee weel, a while!
And I will come again, my luve,
  Tho' it ware ten thousand mile!

ROBERT BURNS

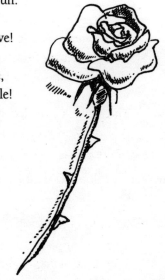

THE HOST OF THE AIR

O'Driscoll drove with a song
The wild duck and the drake
From the tall and the tufted reeds
Of the drear Hart Lake.

And he saw how the reeds grew dark
At the coming of night-tide,
And dreamed of the long dim hair
Of Bridget his bride.

He heard while he sang and dreamed
A piper piping away,
And never was piping so sad,
And never was piping so gay.

And he saw young men and young girls
Who danced on a level place,
And Bridget his bride among them,
With a sad and a gay face.

The dancers crowded about him
And many a sweet thing said,
And a young man brought him red wine
And a young girl white bread.

But Bridget drew him by the sleeve
Away from the merry bands,
To old men playing at cards
With a twinkling of ancient hands.

The bread and the wine had a doom
For these were the host of the air;
He sat and played in a dream
Of her long dim hair.

He played with the merry old men
And thought not of evil chance,
Until one bore Bridget his bride
Away from the merry dance.

He bore her away in his arms,
The handsomest young man there,
And his neck and his breast and his arms
Were drowned in her long dim hair.

O'Driscoll scattered the cards
And out of his dream awoke:
Old men and young men and young girls
Were gone like a drifting smoke;

But he heard high up in the air
A piper piping away,
And never was piping so sad,
And never was piping so gay.

W.B. YEATS

82

ANNABEL LEE

It was many and many a year ago,
    In a kingdom by the sea,
That a maiden there lived whom you may know
    By the name of Annabel Lee;
And this maiden she lived with no other thought
    Than to love and be loved by me.

She was a child and I was a child,
    In this kingdom by the sea;
But we loved with a love that was more than love –
    I and my Annabel Lee;
With a love that the winged seraphs of heaven
    Coveted her and me.

And this was the reason that, long ago,
    In this kingdom by the sea,
A wind blew out of a cloud, chilling
    My beautiful Annabel Lee;
So that her highborn kinsman came
    And bore her away from me,
To shut her up in a sepulchre
    In this kingdom by the sea.

The angels, not half so happy in heaven,
    Went envying her and me –
Yes! – that was the reason (as all men know,
    In this kingdom by the sea)
That the wind came out of the cloud by night,
    Chilling and killing my Annabel Lee.

But our love it was stronger by far than the love
    Of those who were older than we –
    Of many far wiser than we –
And neither the angels in heaven above,
    Nor the demons down under the sea,
Can ever dissever my soul from the soul
    Of the beautiful Annabel Lee.

For the moon never beams without bringing me dreams
    Of the beautiful Annabel Lee;
And the stars never rise but I feel the bright eyes
    Of the beautiful Annabel Lee;
And so, all the night-tide, I lie down by the side
Of my darling – my darling – my life and my bride,
    In the sepulchre there by the sea,
    In her tomb by the sounding sea.

EDGAR ALLAN POE

SHALLOW BROWN

A Yankee ship came down the river
Shallow Shallow Brown
A Yankee ship came down the river
Shallow Shallow Brown
And who do you think was master of her?
Shallow Shallow Brown
And who do you think was master of her?
Shallow Shallow Brown
A Yankee mate and a limejuice skipper
Shallow Shallow Brown
A Yankee mate and a limejuice skipper
Shallow Shallow Brown
And what do you think they had for dinner?
Shallow Shallow Brown
And what do you think they had for dinner?
Shallow Shallow Brown
A parrot's tail and a monkey's liver
Shallow Shallow Brown
A parrot's tail and a monkey's liver
Shallow Shallow Brown

ANONYMOUS

THE CITY PEOPLE MEET THEMSELVES

The city people meet themselves
as they stare in the mirror of the opposite seat.
An old woman smiles at her reflection –
a girl, who's late for work
and urges the train on with a tapping foot –
the crumpled old woman remembers when
her feet tapped to speed up life
but now the feet are tired and old
and each step aches with dwindling hours:
a starched commuter tries not to look
at the broken-down man who cries –
his shallow eyes, pools of hopelessness,
the business man prays that life will be kind
and the treadmill of time will not leave him to cry
in the loneliness of a busy train;
an eager boy gapes at his reflection,
a huge man whose long arms reach to the straps
and smothers the boy in an aura of greatness –
the boy longs for the distant time
when his arms will reach
into the unknown realms of adulthood;
a worn out mother stares across
and sees another woman with the same gaze
grateful for child, but mournful for freedom.
Their eyes meet in silent conversation.

ROSANNE FLYNN

THE SANDS OF DEE

'O Mary, go and call the cattle home,
    And call the cattle home,
    And call the cattle home
  Across the sands of Dee;'
The western wind was wild and dank with foam,
  And all alone went she.

The western tide crept up along the sand,
    And o'er and o'er the sand
    And round and round the sand,
  As far as eye could see.
The rolling mist came down and hid the land;
  And never home came she.

'Oh! is it weed, or fish, or floating hair –
    A tress of golden hair,
    A drowned maiden's hair
  Above the nets at sea?
Was never salmon yet that shone so fair
  Among the stakes on Dee.'

They rowed her in across the rolling foam,
    The cruel crawling foam,
    The cruel hungry foam,
  To her grave beside the sea:
But still the boatmen hear her call the cattle home
  Across the sands of Dee.

CHARLES KINGSLEY

THE THREE TALL MEN

THE FIRST TAPPING

'What's that tapping at night: tack, tack,
In some house in the street at the back?'

'O, 'tis a man who, when he has leisure,
Is making himself a coffin to measure.
He's so very tall that no carpenter
Will make it long enough, he's in fear.
His father's was shockingly short for his limb –
And it made a deep impression on him.'

THE SECOND TAPPING

'That tapping has begun again,
Which ceased a year back, or near then?'

'Yes, 'tis the man you heard before
Making his coffin. The first scarce done
His brother died – his only one –
And, being of his own height, or more,
He used it for him; for he was afraid
He'd not get a long enough one quick made.
He's making a second now, to fit
Himself when there shall be need for it.
Carpenters work so by rule of thumb
That they make mistakes when orders come.'

THE THIRD TAPPING

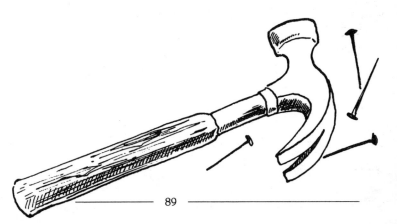

'It's strange, but years back, when I was here,
I used to notice a tapping near;
A man was making his coffin at night,
And he made a second, if I am right?
I have heard again the self-same tapping –
Yes, late last night – or was I napping?'

'O no. It's the same man. He made one
Which his brother had; and a second was done –
For himself, as he thought. But lately his son,
As tall as he, died; aye, and as trim,
And his sorrowful father bestowed it on him.
And now the man is making a third,
To be used for himself when he is interred.'

'Many years later was brought to me
News that the man had died at sea.'

THOMAS HARDY

THE MOLE AND THE EAGLE

The mole is blind, and under ground,
Snug as a nest her home is found;
She dwells secure, nor dreams of sight –
What need of eyes where all is night!

The eagle proudly soars on high,
Bright as the sunbeams is his eye –
To lofty rocks he wings his way,
And sits amid the blaze of day.

The mole needs not the eagle's eye,
Unless she had his wings to fly –
The light of day no joy would give,
If under ground she still must live.

And sad 't would for the eagle be,
If like the mole, he could not see,
Unless you took his wings away,
And shut him from the hope of day.

But both live happy in their way –
One loves the night – and one the day –
And God formed each, and formed their sphere,
And thus his goodness doth appear.

SARAH JOSEPHA HALE

REQUIEM FOR THE CROPPIES

The pockets of our greatcoats full of barley –
No kitchens on the run, no striking camp –
We moved quick and sudden in our own country.
The priest lay behind ditches with the tramp.
A people, hardly marching – on the hike –
We found new tactics happening each day:
We'd cut through reins and rider with the pike
And stampede cattle into infantry,
Then retreat through hedges where cavalry must be thrown.
Until, on Vinegar Hill, the fatal conclave.
Terraced thousands died, shaking scythes at cannon.
The hillside blushed, soaked in our broken wave.
They buried us without shroud or coffin
And in August the barley grew up out of the grave.

SEAMUS HEANEY

A NIGHTMARE

When you're lying awake with a dismal headache, and repose is
    taboo'd by anxiety,
I conceive you may use any language you choose to indulge in without
    impropriety;
For your brain is on fire – the bedclothes conspire of usual slumber to
    plunder you:
First your counterpane goes and uncovers your toes, and your sheet
    slips demurely from under you;
Then the blanketing tickles – you feel like mixed pickles, so terribly
    sharp is the pricking,
And you're hot, and you're cross, and you tumble and toss till there's
    nothing 'twixt you and the ticking.
Then the bedclothes all creep to the ground in a heap, and you pick
    'em all up in a tangle;
Next your pillow resigns and politely declines to remain at its usual
    angle!
Well, you get some repose in the form of a doze, with hot eyeballs and
    head ever aching,
But your slumbering teems with such horrible dreams that you'd very
    much better be waking;

For you dream you are crossing the Channel, and tossing about in a
      steamer from Harwich,
Which is something between a large bathing-machine and a very small
      second-class carriage;
And you're giving a treat (penny ice and cold meat) to a party of
      friends and relations –
They're a ravenous horde – and they all came on board at Sloane
      Square and South Kensington Stations.
And bound on that journey you find your attorney (who started that
      morning from Devon);
He's a bit undersized, and you don't feel surprised when he tells you
      he's only eleven.
Well, you're driving like mad with this singular lad (by the bye the
      ship's now a four-wheeler),
And you're playing round games, and he calls you bad names when you
      tell him that 'ties pay the dealer';
But this you can't stand, so you throw up your hand, and you find
      you're as cold as an icicle,
In your shirt and your socks (the black silk with gold clocks), crossing
      Salisbury Plain on a bicycle:
And he and the crew are on bicycles too – which they've somehow or
      other invested in –
And he's telling the tars all the particulars of a company he's interested
      in –
It's a scheme of devices, to get at low prices, all goods from cough
      mixtures to cables
(Which tickled the sailors) by treating retailers, as though they were all
      vegetables –
You get a good spadesman to plant a small tradesman (first take off his
      boots with a boot-tree),

And his legs will take root, and his fingers will shoot, and they'll
    blossom and bud like a fruit-tree –
From the greengrocer tree you get grapes and green pea, cauliflower,
    pineapple, and cranberries,
While the pastry-cook plant cherry-brandy will grant – apple puffs, and
    three-corners, and banberries –
The shares are a penny, and ever so many are taken by ROTHSCHILD
    and BARING,
And just as a few are allotted to you, you awake with a shudder
    despairing –
You're a regular wreck, with a crick in your neck, and no wonder you
    snore, for your head's on the floor, and you've needles and pins
    from your soles to your shins, and your flesh is a-creep, for your left
    leg's asleep, and you've cramp in your toes, and a fly on your nose,
    and some fluff in your lung, and a feverish tongue, and a thirst that's
    intense, and a general sense that you haven't been sleeping in clover;
But the darkness has passed, and it's daylight at last, and the night
    has been long – ditto, ditto my song – and thank goodness they're
    both of them over!

W. S. GILBERT

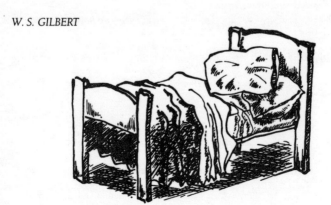

SIX WOMEN

Six women in a chronic ward, the light
Like dirty water filtering away;
Washed, spruced, and fed, they innocently wear
Their flowered shrouds to face the last of day.

One, flapping endlessly, a landed fish,
Thumps on a beach of sheets. One lies and glares
At her reflection in the ceiling's paint,
Writhes to avoid its gaze, and gabbles prayers.

One, deaf as granite, smiles, begins to speak
To someone she, and she alone, has spied;
Calls from the deep and dewy field her cat,
Holds it, invisible, at her clenched side.
One, crouching, poised as if to pounce, stone-still,
Suddenly gives a start, a little squeak:
A mouse-woman with wild and whitened hair,
Dried flakes of tears like snow cooling her cheek.

One, bird-like, lifting up her blinded head
To sounds beyond the television-blare
Cries out, in a sharp sliver of a voice,
I do not know if anyone is there!

I do not know if anyone is here.
If so, if not so, I must let it be.
I hold your drifted hand; no time to tell
What six dead women hear, or whom they see.

CHARLES CAUSLEY

DIGGING

Today I think
Only with scents, – scents dead leaves yield,
And bracken, and wild carrot's seed,
And the square mustard field;

Odours that rise
When the spade wounds the roots of tree,
Rose, currant, raspberry, or goutweed,
Rhubarb or celery;

The smoke's smell, too,
Flowing from where a bonfire burns
The dead, the waste, the dangerous,
And all to sweetness turns.

It is enough
To smell, to crumble the dark earth,
While the robin sings over again
Sad songs of Autumn mirth.

EDWARD THOMAS

THE SMALL WINDOW

In Wales there are jewels
To gather, but with the eye
Only. A hill lights up
Suddenly; a field trembles
With colour and goes out
In its turn; in one day
You can witness the extent
Of the spectrum and grow rich

With looking. Have a care;
This wealth is for the few
And chosen. Those who crowd
A small window dirty it
With their breathing, though sublime
And inexhaustible the view.

R.S. THOMAS

THE CAMEL'S COMPLAINT

Canary-birds feed on sugar and seed,
Parrots have crackers to crunch;
And as for the poodles, they tell me the noodles
Have chicken and cream for their lunch.
But there's never a question
About *my* digestion –
Anything does for me.

Cats, you're aware, can repose in a chair,
Chickens can roost upon rails;
Puppies are able to sleep in a stable,
And oysters can slumber in pails.
But no one supposes
A poor camel dozes –
Any place does for me.

Lambs are enclosed where it's never exposed,
Coops are constructed for hens;
Kittens are treated to houses well heated.
And pigs are protected by pens.
But a camel comes handy
Wherever it's sandy –
Anywhere does for me.

People would laugh if you rode a giraffe,
Or mounted the back of an ox;
It's nobody's habit to ride on a rabbit,
Or try to bestraddle a fox.
But as for a camel, he's
Ridden by families –
Any load does for me.

A snake is as round as a hole in the ground,
And weasels are wavy and sleek;
And no alligator could ever be straighter
Than lizards that live in a creek.
But a camel's all lumpy
And bumpy and humpy –
Any shape does for me.

CHARLES E. CARRYL

SEEN IN PLAIN DAYLIGHT

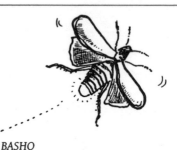

Seen in plain daylight
the firefly's nothing but
an insect

BASHO

BYE, CAT

Cats.
Hate 'em.

All fur and fluff
and spit and eyes in the dark.

Hate them.
Grrr!

At least think I do.
Never caught one.

Always up trees,
or tops of walls,

or leering from windows,
milk on their whiskers,

slipping through hedges
and me on my lead –

always
out of reach.

Never caught one? Never?
A big dog like you? I don't believe a word of it!

OK, I tell a lie
(never told my best friend this).

Caught one once.
Surprised it in the garden.

Up I rushed,
all fangs and claws,

bark like a police siren
promising blue murder.

Didn't move, stupid thing.
Sat there blinking.

What can you do
when a cat won't fight back?

Lick her on the nose.
Bark, 'Got you, kitty.'

Retreat on tip-claw.
'Bye, cat. Bye, cat.'

BRIAN MORSE

SONG OF THE RABBITS OUTSIDE THE TAVERN

We who play under the pines,
We who dance in the snow
That shines blue in the light of the moon
Sometimes halt as we go,
Stand with our ears erect,
Our noses testing the air,
To gaze at the golden world
Behind the windows there.

Suns they have in a cave
And stars each on a tall white stem,
And the thought of fox or night owl
Seems never to trouble them,
They laugh and eat and are warm,
Their food seems ready at hand,
While hungry out in the cold
We little rabbits stand.

But they never dance as we dance,
They have not the speed nor the grace.
We scorn both the cat and the dog
Who lie by their fireplace.
We scorn them licking their paws,
Their eyes on an upraised spoon,
We who dance hungry and wild
Under a winter's moon.

ELIZABETH COATSWORTH

THE FAUN

Ha! sir, I have seen you sniffing and snoozling
    about among my flowers.
And what, pray, do you know about
    horticulture, you capriped?
'Come, Auster, come, Apeliota,
And see the faun in our garden.
But if you move or speak
This thing will run at you
And scare itself to spasms.'

EZRA POUND

LATE AUTUMN

The boy called to his team
    And with blue-glancing share
Turned up the rape and turnip
    With yellow charlock to spare.

The long lean thistles stood
    Like beggars ragged and blind,
Half their white silken locks
    Blown away on the wind.

But I thought not once of winter
    Or summer that was past
Till I saw that slant-legged robin
    With autumn on his chest.

ANDREW YOUNG

JACK

I

Every village has its Jack, but no village ever had
    quite so fine a Jack as ours:-
So picturesque,
Versatile,
Irresponsible,
Powerful,
Hedonistic,
And lovable a Jack as ours.

II

How Jack lived none know, for he rarely did any work.
True, he set night-lines for eels, and invariably caught one,
Often two,
Sometimes three;
While very occasionally he had a day's harvesting or hay-making.
And yet he always found enough money for tobacco,
With a little over for beer, though he was no soaker.

III

Jack had a wife.
A soulless, savage woman she was, who disapproved
    volubly of his idle ways.
But the only result was to make him stay out longer,
(Like Rip van Winkle).

IV

Jack had a big black beard, and a red shirt, which was made for
    another.
And no waistcoat.
His boots were somebody else's;
He wore the Doctor's coat,
And the Vicar's trousers.
Personally, I gave him a hat, but it was too small.

V

Everybody liked Jack.
The Vicar liked him, although he never went to church.
Indeed, he was a cheerful Pagan, with no temptation
    to break more than the Eighth Commandment,
    and no ambition as a sinner.
The Curate liked him, although he had no simpering daughters.
The Doctor liked him, although he was never ill.
I liked him too – chiefly because of his perpetual
    good temper, and his intimacy with Nature, and
    his capacity for colouring cutties.
The girls liked him, because he brought them the
    first wild roses and the sweetest honeysuckle;
Also, because he could flatter so outrageously.

VI

But the boys loved him.
They followed him in little bands:
Jack was their hero.

And no wonder, for he could hit a running rabbit with a stone.
And cut them long, straight fishing poles and equilateral catty
    forks.
And he always knew of a fresh nest.
Besides, he could make a thousand things with his old pocket-
    knife.

VII

How good he was at cricket too!
On the long summer evenings he would saunter to the
    green and watch the lads at play,
And by and by someone would offer him a few knocks.
Then the Doctor's coat would be carefully detached,
    and Jack would spit on his hands, and brandish the bat,
And away the ball would go, north and south, and east and west,
And sometimes bang into the zenith.
For Jack had little science:
Upon each ball he made the same terrific and magnificent
    onslaught,
Whether half-volley, or full pitch, or long hop, or
    leg break, or off break, or shooter, or yorker.
And when the stumps fell he would cheerfully set them
    up again, while his white teeth flashed
    in the recesses of his beard.

VIII

The only persons who were not conspicuously fond of Jack
    were his wife, and the schoolmaster and
    the head-keeper.
The schoolmaster had an idea that if Jack were
    hanged there would be no more truants;
His wife would attend the funeral without an
    extraordinary show of grief;
And the head-keeper would mutter, 'There's one
    poacher less.'

IX

Jack was quite as much a part of the village as the church spire;
And if any of us lazied along by the river in the dusk of the
    evening –
Waving aside nebulae of gnats,
Turning head quickly at the splash of a jumping fish,
Peering where the water chuckled over a vanishing water rat –
And saw not Jack's familiar form bending over his lines,
And smelt not his vile shag,
We should feel a loneliness, a vague impression that something
    was wrong.

X

For ten years Jack was always the same,
Never growing older,
Or richer,
Or tidier,
Never knowing that we had a certain pride in possessing him.
Then there came a tempter with tales of easily acquired
    wealth, and Jack went away in his company.

XI

He has never come back,
And now the village is like a man who has lost an eye.
In the gloaming, no slouching figure, with colossal
    idleness in every line, leans against my
    garden wall, with prophecies of the morrow's weather;
And those who reviled Jack most wonder now
    what it was they found fault with.
We feel our bereavement deeply.
The Vicar, I believe, would like to offer public prayer
    for the return of the wanderer.
And the Doctor, I know, is a little unhinged, and
    curing people out of pure absence of mind.
For my part, I have hope; and the trousers I
    discarded last week will not be given
    away just yet.

E. V. LUCAS

THE BATTLE HYMN OF THE REPUBLIC

Mine eyes have seen the glory of the coming of the Lord:
He is trampling out the vintage where the grapes of wrath are
    stored;
He hath loosed the fatal lightning of His terrible swift sword:
      His truth is marching on.

I have seen Him in the watch-fires of a hundred circling camps,
They have builded Him an altar in the evening dews and damps;
I can read His righteous sentence by the dim and flaring lamps:
      His day is marching on.

I have read a fiery gospel writ in burnished rows of steel:
'As ye deal with my contemners, so with you my grace shall deal;
Let the Hero, born of woman, crush the serpent with his heel,
      Since God is marching on.'

He has sounded forth the trumpet that shall never call retreat;
He is sifting out the hearts of men before His judgement seat:
Oh, be swift, my soul, to answer Him! Be jubilant, my feet!
      Our God is marching on.

In the beauty of the lilies Christ was born across the sea,
With a glory in his bosom that transfigures you and me:
As he died to make men holy, let us die to make men free,
      While God is marching on.

JULIA WARD HOWE

A TRAGIC STORY

There lived a sage in days of yore,
And he a handsome pigtail wore:
But wondered much, and sorrowed more,
  Because it hung behind him.

He mused upon this curious case,
And swore he'd change the pigtail's place,
And have it hanging at his face,
  Not dangling there behind him.

Says he, 'The mystery I've found –
I'll turn me round,'
He turned him round;
  But still it hung behind him.

Then round, and round, and out and in,
All day the puzzled sage did spin;
In vain – it mattered not a pin –
  The pigtail hung behind him.

And right and left, and round about,
And up and down, and in and out,
He turned; but still the pigtail stout
  Hung steadily behind him.

And though his efforts never slack
And though he twist, and twirl, and tack,
Alas! still faithful to his back,
  The pigtail hangs behind him.

WILLIAM MAKEPEACE THACKERAY

LUCKY ME

Grass and carrots for the rabbit,
Seeds and grain for the turkey,
Some parboiled figs
Will do for the pigs,
But all the best foods for me.

One tiny hutch for the rabbit,
One little coop for the turkey,
I can't think why
Pigs love a sty,
But it's a nice big house for me.

They make a stew out of the rabbit,
And Christmas dinner from the turkey,
Pigs are taken
For ham and bacon,
But nobody dares eat me.

VALERIE BLOOM

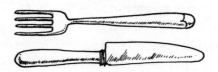

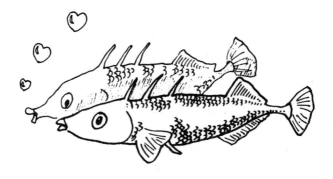

STICKLEBACK

The Stickleback's a spiky chap,
    Worse than a bit of briar.
Hungry Pike would sooner swallow
    Embers from a fire.

The Stickleback is fearless in
    The way he loves his wife.
Every minute of the day
    He guards her with his life.

She, like him, is dressed to kill
    In stiff and steely prickles,
And when they kiss, there bubbles up
    The laughter of the tickles.

TED HUGHES

LONG, LONG AGO

It seems I always saw the Indian woman
the instant she became visible,
and never took my eyes off her
as she lugged her many-coloured pack,
three times as big as herself,
down South Mountain,
across Little Bridge,
up North Mountain
and into our kitchen
where she undid a knot
and flooded the entire room with baskets
– cherry-coloured baskets,
wheat-coloured baskets,
cabbage-coloured baskets,
baskets the colour of a November sky,
each basket containing
another, smaller basket,
down to one so tiny it would hold
only a hang of thread and a thimble.

ALDEN NOWLAN

JAMAICAN BUS RIDE

The live fowl squatting on the grapefruit and bananas
in the basket of the copper-coloured lady
is gloomy but resigned.
The four very large baskets on the floor
are in everybody's way,
as the conductor points out
loudly, often, but in vain.

Two quadroon dandies are disputing
who is standing on whose feet.

When we stop,
a boy vanishes through the door marked ENTRANCE;
but those entering through the door marked EXIT
are greatly hindered by the fact that when we started
there were twenty standing,
and another ten have somehow inserted themselves
into invisible crannies
between dark and sweating body and body.

With an odour of petrol
both excessive and alarming
we hurtle hell-for-leather
between crimson bougainvillea blossom
and scarlet poinsettia
and miraculously do not run over
three goats, seven hens and a donkey
as we pray
that the driver has not fortified himself

at Daisy's Drinking Saloon
with more than four rums:
or by the gods of Jamaica
this day is our last!

A.S.J. TESSIMOND

THE CHARGE OF THE LIGHT BRIGADE

Half a league, half a league,
   Half a league onward,
All in the valley of Death
   Rode the six hundred.
'Forward, the Light Brigade!
Charge for the guns!' he said;
Into the valley of Death
   Rode the six hundred.

'Forward, the Light Brigade!'
Was there a man dismayed?
Not tho' the soldier knew
   Some one had blundered:
Theirs not to make reply,
Theirs not to reason why,
Theirs but to do and die:
Into the valley of Death
   Rode the six hundred.

Cannon to right of them,
Cannon to left of them,
Cannon in front of them
   Volleyed and thundered;
Stormed at with shot and shell,
Boldly they rode and well,
Into the jaws of Death,
Into the mouth of Hell
   Rode the six hundred.

Flashed all their sabres bare,
Flashed as they turned in air,
Sabring the gunners there,
Charging an army, while
  All the world wondered:
Plunged in the battery-smoke
Right thro' the line they broke;
Cossack and Russian
Reeled from the sabre-stroke
  Shattered and sundered.
Then they rode back, but not,
  Not the six hundred.

Cannon to right of them,
Cannon to left of them,
Cannon behind them
  Volleyed and thundered;
Stormed at with shot and shell,
While horse and hero fell,
They that had fought so well
Came thro' the jaws of Death
Back from the mouth of Hell,
All that was left of them,
  Left of six hundred.

When can their glory fade?
O the wild charge they made!
  All the world wondered.
Honour the charge they made!
Honour the Light Brigade,
  Noble six hundred!

ALFRED, LORD TENNYSON

I ASKED THE LITTLE BOY WHO CANNOT SEE

I asked the little boy who cannot see,
'And what is colour like?'
'Why, green,' said he,
'Is like the rustle when the wind blows through
The forest; running water, that is blue;
And red is like a trumpet sound; and pink
Is like the smell of roses; and I think
That purple must be like a thunderstorm;
And yellow is like something soft and warm;
And white is a pleasant stillness when you lie
And dream.'

ANONYMOUS

OLD PEOPLE

Why are people impatient when they are old?
Is it because they are tired of trying to make
Fast things move slowly?
I have seen their eyes flinch as they watch the lorries
Lurching and hurrying past.
I have also seen them twitch and move away
When a grandbaby cries.
They can go to the cinema cheaply,
They can do what they like all day.
Yet they shrink and shiver, looking like old, used dolls.
I do not think that I should like to be old.

ELIZABETH JENNINGS

THE CHOIRMASTER'S BURIAL

He often would ask us
That, when he died,
After playing so many
To their last rest,
If out of us any
Should here abide,
And it would not task us,
We would with our lutes
Play over him
By his grave-brim
The psalm he liked best –
The one whose sense suits
'Mount Ephraim' –
And perhaps we should seem
To him, in Death's dream,
Like the seraphim.

As soon as I knew
That his spirit was gone
I thought this his due,
And spoke thereupon.

'I think,' said the vicar,
'A read service quicker
Than viols out-of-doors
In these frosts and hoars.
That old-fashioned way
Requires a fine day,
And it seems to me
It had better not be.'

Hence, that afternoon,
Though never knew he
That his wish could not be,
To get through it faster
They buried the master
Without any tune.

But 'twas said that, when
At the dead of next night
The vicar looked out,
There struck on his ken
Thronged roundabout,
Where the frost was greying
The headstoned grass,
A band all in white
Like the saints in church-glass,
Singing and playing
The ancient stave
By the choirmaster's grave.

Such the tenor man told
When he had grown old.

THOMAS HARDY

SAD AUNT MADGE

As the cold winter evenings drew near
Aunt Madge used to put extra blankets
over the furniture, to keep it warm and cosy
Mussolini was her lover, and life
was an outoffocus rosy-tinted spectacle

but neurological experts
with kind blueeyes
and gentle voices
small white hands
and large Rolls Royces
said that electric shock treatment
should do the trick
it did ...

today after 15 years of therapeutic tears
and an awful lot of ratepayers' shillings
down the hospital meter
sad Aunt Madge
no longer tucks up the furniture
before kissing it goodnight
and admits
that her affair with Mussolini
clearly was not right
particularly in the light
of her recently announced engagement
to the late pope.

ROGER McGOUGH

ROMAN WALL BLUES

Over the heather the wet wind blows,
I've lice in my tunic and a cold in my nose.

The rain comes pattering out of the sky,
I'm a Wall soldier, I don't know why.

The mist creeps over the hard grey stone,
My girl's in Tungria; I sleep alone.

Aulus goes hanging around her place,
I don't like his manners, I don't like his face.

Piso's a Christian, he worships a fish;
There'd be no kissing if he had his wish.

She gave me a ring but I diced it away;
I want my girl and I want my pay.

When I'm a veteran with only one eye
I shall do nothing but look at the sky.

W.H. AUDEN

CONSERVATION PIECE

The countryside must be preserved!
(Preferably miles away from me.)
Neat hectares of the stuff reserved
For those in need of flower or tree.

I'll make do with landscape painting
Film documentaries on TV
And when I need to escape, panting,
Then open-mouthed I'll head for the sea.

Let others stroll and take their leisure,
In grasses wade up to their knees,
For I derive no earthly pleasure
From the green green rash that makes me sneeze.

ROGER McGOUGH

WINTER MAGIC

A crumb of bread,
For such expenditure I've been repaid
With three clear silvery notes,
Three lingering notes,
Trilled from the little throat
Of one small bird,
And all the frost-bound earth
At once burst forth
In flowers of Spring,
And bridal dresses robed the trees
Tissued with sprays of blush-white blossom,
And the air was heavy
With the fresh earth's smell
And drowsy with the hum of honey bees –
Such magic lies in three clear rippling notes
Trilled by a little bird
In thanksgiving
For one small crumb of bread.

ANONYMOUS

POEM

As the cat
climbed over
the top of

the jamcloset
first the right
forefoot

carefully
then the hind
stepped down

into the pit of
the empty
flowerpot

WILLIAM CARLOS WILLIAMS

JACK FROST

Rustily creak the crickets: Jack Frost came down last night,
He slid to the earth on a starbeam, keen and sparkling and bright;
He sought in the grass for the crickets with delicate icy spear,
So sharp and fine and fatal, and he stabbed them far and near.
Only a few stout fellows, thawed by the morning sun,
Chirrup a mournful echo of by-gone frolic and fun.
But yesterday such a rippling chorus ran all over the land,
Over the hills and the valleys, down to the grey sea-sand
Millions of merry harlequins, skipping and dancing in glee,
Cricket and locust and grasshopper, happy as happy could be:
Scooping rich caves in ripe apples, and feeding on honey and
    spice,
Drunk with the mellow sunshine, nor dreaming of spears of ice!
Was it not enough that the crickets your weapon of power should
    pierce?
Pray what have you done to the flowers? Jack Frost, you are cruel
    and fierce.
With never a sign or a whisper, you kissed them and lo, they
    exhale
Their beautiful lives; they are drooping, their sweet colour ebbs,
    they are pale,
They fade and they die! See the pansies, yet striving so hard to
    unfold
Their garments of velvety splendour, all Tyrian purple and gold.
But now weary they look, and how withered, like handsome court
    dames, who all night
Have danced at the ball till the sunrise struck chill to their
    hearts with its light.
Where hides the wood-aster? She vanished as snow wreaths dissolve
    in the sun

The moment you touched her. Look yonder, where sober and grey as a nun,
The maple-tree stands that at sunset was blushing and red as the
    sky;
At its foot, glowing scarlet as fire, its robes of magnificence
    lie.
Despoiler! stripping the world as you strip the shivering tree
Of colour and sound and perfume, scaring the bird and the bee,
Turning beauty to ashes – oh to join the swift swallows and fly
Far away out of sight of your mischief! I give you no welcome,
    not I!

CELIA THAXTER

SYMPHONY IN YELLOW

An omnibus across the bridge
  Crawls like a yellow butterfly,
  And, here and there, a passer-by
Shows like a little restless midge.

Big barges full of yellow hay
  Are moored against the shadowy wharf,
  And, like a yellow silken scarf,
The thick fog hangs along the quay.

The yellow leaves begin to fade
  And flutter from the Temple elms,
  And at my feet the pale green Thames
Lies like a rod of rippled jade.

OSCAR WILDE

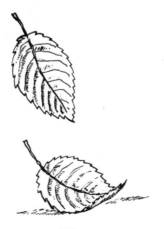

NATURE

We have neither Summer nor Winter
Neither Autumn nor Spring.
We have instead the days
When the gold sun shines on the lush green canefields –
Magnificently.
The days when the rain beats like bullets on the roofs
And there is no sound but the swish of water in the gullies
And trees struggling in the high Jamaica winds.
Also there are the days when leaves fade from off guango trees
And the reaped canefields lie bare and fallow to the sun.
But best of all there are the days when the mango and the
    logwood blossom
When the bushes are full of the sound of bees and the scent of
    honey,
When the tall grass sways and shivers to the slightest breath of
    air,
When the buttercups have paved the earth with yellow stars
And beauty comes suddenly and the rains have gone.

H. D. CARBERRY

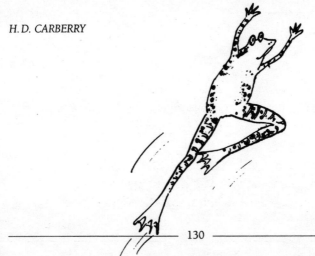

THE TREES ARE DOWN

They are cutting down the great plane-trees at the end of the
    gardens.
For days there has been the grate of the saw, the swish of the
    branches as they fall,
The crash of the trunks, the rustle of trodden leaves,
With the 'Whoops' and the 'Whoas', the loud common talk,
    the loud common laughs of the men, above it all.

I remember one evening of a long past Spring
Turning in at a gate, getting out of a cart, and finding a large
    dead rat in the mud of the drive.
I remember thinking: alive or dead, a rat was a god-forsaken
    thing,
But at least, in May, that even a rat should be alive.

The week's work here is as good as done. There is just one
    bough
  On the roped bole, in the fine grey rain,
    Green and high
    And lonely against the sky.
      (Down now!–)
    And but for that,
    If an old dead rat
Did once, for a moment, unmake the Spring, I might never
    have thought of him again.

It is not for a moment the Spring is unmade to-day;
These were great trees, it was in them from root to stem:
When the men with the 'Whoops' and the 'Whoas' have

    carted the whole of the whispering loveliness away
Half the Spring, for me, will have gone with them.

It is going now, and my heart has been struck with the hearts
    of the planes;
Half my life it has beat with these, in the sun, in the rains,
  In the March wind, the May breeze,
In the great gales that came over to them across the roofs
    from the great seas.
    There was only a quiet rain when they were dying;
    They have heard the sparrows flying,
And the small creeping creatures in the earth where they were
    lying –
    But I, all day, I heard an angel crying:
    'Hurt not the trees.'

CHARLOTTE MEW

DOVER BEACH

The sea is calm to-night.
The tide is full, the moon lies fair
Upon the straits; – on the French coast the light
Gleams and is gone; the cliffs of England stand,
Glimmering and vast, out in the tranquil bay.
Come to the window, sweet is the night-air!
Only, from the long line of spray
Where the sea meets the moon-blanched land,
Listen! you hear the grating roar
Of pebbles which the waves draw back, and fling,
At their return, up the high strand,
Begin, and cease, and then again begin,
With tremulous cadence slow, and bring
The eternal note of sadness in.

Sophocles long ago
Heard it on the Aegæan, and it brought
Into his mind the turbid ebb and flow
Of human misery; we
Find also in the sound a thought,
Hearing it by this distant northern sea.

The Sea of Faith
Was once, too, at the full, and round earth's shore
Lay like the folds of a bright girdle furled.
But now I only hear
Its melancholy, long, withdrawing roar,
Retreating, to the breath
Of the night-wind, down the vast edges drear
And naked shingles of the world.

Ah, love, let us be true
To one another! for the world, which seems
To lie before us like a land of dreams,
So various, so beautiful, so new,
Hath really neither joy, nor love, nor light,
Nor certitude, nor peace, nor help for pain;
And we are here as on a darkling plain
Swept with confused alarms of struggle and flight,
Where ignorant armies clash by night.

MATTHEW ARNOLD

'I STARTED EARLY – TOOK MY DOG'

I started Early – Took my Dog –
And visited the Sea –
The Mermaids in the Basement
Came out to look at me –

And Frigates – in the Upper Floor
Extended Hempen Hands –
Presuming Me to be a Mouse –
Aground – upon the Sands –

But no Man moved Me – till the Tide
Went past my simple Shoe –
And past my Apron – and my Belt
And past my Bodice – too –
And made as He would eat me up –
As wholly as a Dew
Upon a Dandelion's Sleeve –
And then – I started – too –

And He – He followed – close behind –
I felt His Silver Heel
Upon my Ankle –Then my Shoes
Would overflow with Pearl –

Until We met the Solid Town –
No One He seemed to know –
And bowing – with a Mighty look –
At me –The Sea withdrew –

EMILY DICKINSON

WHO WILL GO FIRST?

We'll go first, said the ants
Because we are the smallest.

No, I'll go first, said Elephant
Because I'm the heaviest.

Sorry, but I'll go first, said the
Monkey.

No, said Noah
Giraffe is first, because his neck
has been hurting.

KEVIN HORTED

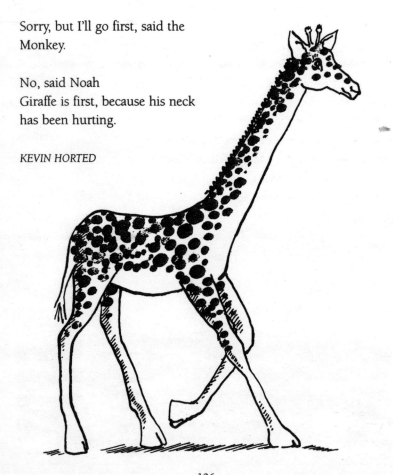

SQUIRRELS IN MY NOTEBOOK

I went to Stanley Park
to put squirrels in my notebook
My teacher said
write everything you found out
about squirrels

and so I will

I saw a fat one
shaped like a peanut butter jar
attacking my hat

his moustache was made of chips
he ran sideways into the sky

He looked like a ginger cat
with a branch for a tail

He was so mad he ran down again
and I can't write
what he said to me

Lucky for me I had a sandwich
to share with him

He smiled at me till his teeth
weren't hungry
and jumped into the sky
with his jammy legs
he turned into
a kite.

FLORENCE McNEIL

THE SOUND OF THE WIND

The wind has such a rainy sound
  Moaning through the town,
The sea has such a windy sound –
  Will the ships go down?

The apples in the orchard
  Tumble from their tree –
Oh will the ships go down, go down,
  In the windy sea?

CHRISTINA ROSSETTI

NO!

No sun – no moon!
No morn – no noon –
No dawn – no dusk – no proper time of day –
No sky – no earthly view –
No distance looking blue –
No road – no street – no 't'other side the way' –
No end to any Row –
No indications where the Crescents go –
No top to any steeple –
No recognitions of familiar people –
No courtesies for showing 'em –
No knowing 'em! –
No travelling at all – no locomotion,
No inkling of the way – no notion –
No go; – by land or ocean –
No mail – no post –
No news from any foreign coast –
No Park – no Ring – no afternoon gentility –
No company – no nobility –
No warmth, no cheerfulness, no healthful ease,
No comfortable feel in any member –
No shade, no shine, no butterflies, no bees,
No fruits, no flowers, no leaves, no birds –
November!

THOMAS HOOD

SHALLOW POEM

I've thought of a poem.
I carry it carefully,
nervously, in my head,
like a saucer of milk;
in case I should spill some lines
before I can put it down.

GERDA MAYER

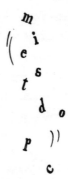

HOW TO GET ON IN SOCIETY

Phone for the fish-knives, Norman
    As Cook is a little unnerved;
You kiddies have crumpled the serviettes
    And I must have things daintily served.

Are the requisites all in the toilet?
    The frills round the cutlets can wait
Till the girl has replenished the cruets
    And switched on the logs in the grate.

It's ever so close in the lounge, dear,
    But the vestibule's comfy for tea
And Howard is out riding on horseback
    So do come and take some with me.

Now here is a fork for your pastries
    And do use the couch for your feet;
I know what I wanted to ask you –
    Is trifle sufficient for sweet?

Milk and then just as it comes dear?
    I'm afraid the preserve's full of stones;
Beg pardon, I'm soiling the doileys
    With afternoon tea-cakes and scones.

JOHN BETJEMAN

I MET AT EVE

I met at eve the Prince of Sleep,
His was a still and lovely face,
He wandered through a valley steep,
  Lovely in a lonely place.

His garb was grey of lavender,
About his brows a poppy-wreath
Burned like dim coals, and everywhere
  The air was sweeter for his breath.

His twilight feet no sandals wore,
His eyes shone faint in their own flame,
Fair moths that gloomed his steps before
  Seemed letters of his lovely name.

His house is in the mountain ways,
A phantom house of misty walls,
Whose golden flocks at evening graze,
  And 'witch the moon with muffled calls.

Upwelling from his shadowy springs
Sweet waters shake a trembling sound,
There flit the hoot-owl's silent wings,
  There hath his web the silkworm wound.

Dark in his pools clear visions lurk,
And rosy, as with morning buds,
Along his dales of broom and birk
  Dreams haunt his solitary woods.

I met at eve the Prince of Sleep,
His was a still and lovely face,
He wandered through a valley steep
  Lovely in a lonely place.

WALTER DE LA MARE

THE IDLERS

The gipsies lit their fires by the chalk-pit gate anew,
And the hoppled horses supped in the further dusk and dew;
The gnats flocked round the smoke like idlers as they were
And through the goss and bushes the owls began to churr.

An ell above the woods the last of sunset glowed
With a dusky gold that filled the pond beside the road;
The cricketers had done, the leas all silent lay,
And the carrier's clattering wheels went past and died
    away.

The gipsies lolled and gossiped, and ate their stolen swedes,
Made merry with mouth-organs, worked toys with piths of
    reeds:
The old wives puffed their pipes, nigh as black as their
    hair,
And not one of them all seemed to know the name of care.

EDMUND BLUNDEN

DIVALI

Winter stalks us
like a leopard in the mountains
scenting prey.

It grows dark,
bare trees stick black bars
across the moon's silver eye.

I will light my lamp for you
Lakshmi,
drive away the darkness.

Welcome you into my home
Lakshmi,
beckon you from every window

With light that blazes
out like flames
across the sombre sky.

Certain houses
crouch in shadow, do not hear
your gentle voice.

Will not feel
your gentle heartbeat
bring prosperity and fortune.

Darkness hunts them
like a leopard in the mountains
stalking prey.

DAVID HARMER

ELEGY ON THE DEATH OF A MAD DOG

Good people all, of every sort,
  Give ear unto my song;
And if you find it wondrous short,
  It cannot hold you long.

In Islington there was a man,
  Of whom the world might say,
That still a godly race he ran,
  Whene'er he went to pray.

A kind and gentle heart he had,
  To comfort friends and foes;
The naked every day he clad,
  When he put on his clothes.

And in that town a dog was found,
  As many dogs there be,
Both mongrel, puppy, whelp, and hound,
  And curs of low degree.

This dog and man at first were friends;
  But when a pique began,
The dog, to gain some private ends,
  Went mad and bit the man.

Around from all the neighbouring streets
  The wondering neighbours ran,
And swore the dog had lost his wits,
  To bite so good a man.

The wound it seemed both sore and sad
  To every Christian eye;
And while they swore the dog was mad,
  They swore the man would die.

But soon a wonder came to light,
  That showed the rogues they lied:
The man recovered of the bite –
  The dog it was that died.

OLIVER GOLDSMITH

THE POPLAR FIELD

The poplars are fell'd, farewell to the shade
And the whispering sound of the cool colonnade:
The winds play no longer and sing in the leaves,
Nor Ouse on his bosom their image receives.

Twelve years have elapsed since I first took a view
Of my favourite field, and the bank where they grew:
And now in the grass behold they are laid,
And the tree is my seat that once lent me a shade.

The blackbird has fled to another retreat
Where the hazels afford him a screen from the heat;
And the scene where his melody charm'd me before
Resounds with his sweet-flowing ditty no more.

My fugitive years are all hasting away,
And I must ere long lie as lowly as they,
With a turf on my breast and a stone at my head,
Ere another such grove shall arise in its stead.

'Tis a sight to engage me, if anything can,
To muse on the perishing pleasures of man;
Short-lived as we are, our enjoyments, I see,
Have a still shorter date, and die sooner than we.

WILLIAM COWPER

'HOPE' IS THE THING WITH FEATHERS

'Hope' is the thing with feathers –
That perches in the soul –
And sings the tune without the words –
And never stops – at all –

And sweetest – in the Gale – is heard –
And sore must be the storm –
That could abash the little Bird
That kept so many warm –

I've heard it in the chillest land –
And on the strangest Sea –
Yet, never, in Extremity,
It asked a crumb – of Me.

EMILY DICKINSON

MY MOCCASINS HAVE NOT WALKED

My moccasins have not walked
Among the giant forest trees

My leggings have not brushed
Against the fern and berry bush

My medicine pouch has not been filled
With roots and herbs and sweetgrass

My hands have not fondled the spotted fawn

My eyes have not beheld
The golden rainbow of the north

My hair has not been adorned
With the eagle feather

Yet
My dreams are dreams of these
My heart is one with them
The scent of them caresses my soul

DUKE REDBIRD

HIGHEST PRICE

'Who will buy me, who will buy me, rid me of my cares?'
Thus I shout and thus I wander through my nights and days;
    And with each day that passes
    My basket presses
    Upon my head more heavily.
People come and go: some laugh; some watch me tearfully.

At noon I make my way along the king's great stone-paved road,
And soon he comes in his chariot, sword in hand, crown on his
    head.
    'I'll buy by force,' he says
    And grabs me, tries
    To drag me off. I wriggle free
With ease; the king climbs into his golden chariot and rides away.

In small back lanes I wander past bolted and shuttered doors.
A door opens; an old man with a money-bag appears.
    He examines what I have
    And says, 'I'll give
    You gold.' He returns again and again,
Empties his purse. With far-off thoughts I carry my basket on.

At evening over the richly blossoming forest moonbeams fall.
Near to the base of a bakul-tree I meet a beautiful girl.
    She edges close: 'My smile
    Will make you sell,'
    She says. Her smile soon turns to weeping.
Slowly, softly she moves away into the woodland gloaming.

Along the sea-shore the sun shines, the sea breaks and rolls.
A child is on the sandy beach: he sits playing with shells.

   He seems to know me; he says,

   'I'll buy your cares

   For nothing.' Suddenly I am released

From my heavy load; his playful face has won me free of cost.

RABINDRANATH TAGORE

EXTRACT FROM THE BOOK OF ECCLESIASTES

To every thing there is a season,

   and a time to every purpose under heaven:

A time to be born, and a time to die;

   a time to plant, and a time to pluck up that which is planted;

A time to kill, and a time to heal;

   a time to break down, and a time to build up;

A time to weep, and a time to laugh;

   a time to mourn, and a time to dance;

A time to cast away stones, and a time to gather stones together;

   a time to embrace, and a time to refrain from embracing;

A time to get, and a time to lose;

   a time to keep, and a time to cast away;

A time to rend, and a time to sew;

   a time to keep silence, and a time to speak;

   A time to love, and a time to hate;

   a time of war, and a time of peace.

THE BLIND MEN AND THE ELEPHANT

It was six men of Indostan
    To learning much inclined,
Who went to see the Elephant
    (Though all of them were blind),
That each by observation
    Might satisfy his mind.

The First approached the Elephant,
    And happening to fall
Against his broad and sturdy side,
    At once began to bawl:
'God bless me! but the Elephant
    Is very like a wall!'

The Second, feeling of the tusk,
    Cried, 'Ho! what have we here
So very round and smooth and sharp?
    To me 'tis mighty clear
This wonder of an Elephant
    Is very like a spear!'

The Third approached the animal,
    And happening to take
The squirming trunk within his hands,
    Thus boldly up and spake:
'I see,' quoth he, 'the Elephant
    Is very like a snake!'

The Fourth reached out an eager hand,
    And felt about the knee.
'What most this wondrous beast is like
    Is mighty plain,' quoth he;
''Tis clear enough the Elephant
    Is very like a tree!'

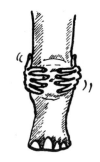

The Fifth who chanced to touch the ear,
    Said: 'E'en that blindest man
Can tell what this resembles most;
    Deny the fact who can,
This marvel of an Elephant
    Is very like a fan!'

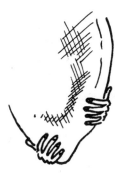

The Sixth no sooner had begun
    About the beast to grope,
Than, seizing on the swinging tail
    That fell within his scope,
'I see,' quoth he, 'the Elephant
    Is very like a rope!'

And so these men of Indostan
    Disputed loud and long,
Each in his own opinion
    Exceeding stiff and strong,
Though each was partly in the right,
    And all were in the wrong!

Moral

So oft in theologic wars,
　　The disputants, I ween,
Rail on in utter ignorance
　　Of what each other mean,
And prate about an Elephant
　　Not one of them has seen!

JOHN GODFREY SAXE

BLAKE LEADS A WALK ON THE MILKY WAY

He gave silver shoes to the rabbit
and golden gloves to the cat
and emerald boots to the tiger and me
and boots of iron to the rat.

He enquired, 'Is everyone ready?
The night is uncommonly cold.
We'll start on our journey as children,
but I fear we will finish it old.'

He hurried us to the horizon
where morning and evening meet.
The slippery stars went skipping
under our hapless feet.

'I'm terribly cold,' said the rabbit.
'my paws are becoming quite blue,
and what will become of my right thumb
while you admire the view?'

'The stars,' said the cat, 'are abundant
and falling on every side.
Let them carry us back to our comforts.
Let us take the stars for a ride.'

'I shall garland my room,' said the tiger,
'with a few of these emerald lights.'
'I shall give up sleeping forever,' I said.
'I shall never part day from night.'

The rat was sullen. He grumbled
he ought to have stayed in his bed.
'What's gathered by fools in heaven
will never endure,' he said.

Blake gave silver stars to the rabbit
and golden stars to the cat
and emerald stars to the tiger and me
but a handful of dirt to the rat.

NANCY WILLARD

MEDITATIO

When I carefully consider the curious habits of dogs
I am compelled to conclude
That man is the superior animal.

When I consider the curious habits of man
I confess, my friend, I am puzzled.

EZRA POUND

MY BOY JACK

'Have you news of my boy Jack?'
    Not this tide.
'When d'think that he'll come back?'
    Not with this wind blowing, and this tide.

'Has anyone else had word of him?'
    Not this tide.
For what is sunk will hardly swim,
    Not with this wind blowing and this tide.

'Oh, dear, what comfort can I find?'
    Not this tide,
    Nor any tide,
Except he did not shame his kind –
    Not even with that wind blowing, and that tide.

Then hold your head up all the more,
    This tide,
    And every tide;
Because he was the son you bore,
    And gave to that wind blowing and that tide!

RUDYARD KIPLING

THE LAKE

For years there have been no fish in the lake.
People hurrying through the park avoid it
like the plague. Birds steer clear
and the sedge of course has withered.
Trees lean away from it,
and at night it reflects, not the moon,
but the blackness of its own depths.
There are no fish in the lake.
But there is life there. There is life ...

Underwater pigs glide between reefs of coral debris.
They love it here. They breed and multiply
in sties hollowed out of the mud
and lined with mattresses and bedsprings.
They live on dead fish and rotting things,
drowned pets, plastic and assorted excreta.
Rusty cans they like the best.
Holding them in webbed trotters
their teeth tear easily through the tin,

and poking in a snout, they noisily suck out
the putrid matter within.
There are no fish in the lake.
But there is life there. There is life ...

For on certain evenings after dark
shoals of pigs surface
and look out at those houses near the park.
Where, in bathrooms,
children feed stale bread to plastic ducks,
and in attics,
toy yachts have long since run aground.
Where, in livingrooms,
anglers dangle their lines on patterned carpets,
and bemoan the fate of the ones that got away.

Down on the lake, piggy eyes glisten.
They have acquired a taste for flesh.
They are licking their lips. Listen ...

ROGER McGOUGH

MY TRUE LOVE HATH MY HEART

My true love hath my heart, and I have his,
By just exchange one for the other given.
I hold his dear, and mine he cannot miss:
There never was a better bargain driven.
His heart in me keeps me and him in one;
My heart in him his thoughts and senses guides;
He loves my heart, for once it was his own;
I cherish his, because in me it bides.
His heart his wound received from my sight;
My heart was wounded with his wounded heart;
For as from me on him his hurt did light,
So still, me thought, in me his hurt did smart;
     Both equal hurt, in this change sought our bliss:
     My true love hath my heart, and I have his.

SIR PHILIP SIDNEY

AND DID THOSE FEET IN ANCIENT TIME

And did those feet in ancient time
Walk upon England's mountains green?
And was the holy lamb of God
On England's pleasant pastures seen?

And did the countenance divine
Shine forth upon our clouded hills?
And was Jerusalem builded here
Among those dark satanic mills?

Bring me my bow of burning gold:
Bring me my arrows of desire:
Bring me my spear: O clouds unfold!
Bring me my chariot of fire.

I will not cease from mental fight,
Nor shall my sword sleep in my hand
Till we have built Jerusalem
In England's green and pleasant land.

WILLIAM BLAKE

ON A NIGHT OF SNOW

Cat, if you go outdoors, you must walk in the snow.
You will come back with little white shoes on your feet,
little white shoes of snow that have heels of sleet.
Stay by the fire, my Cat. Lie still, do not go.
See how the flames are leaping and hissing low,
I will bring you a saucer of milk like a marguerite,
so white and so smooth, so spherical and so sweet –
stay with me, Cat. Outdoors the wild winds blow.

Outdoors the wild winds blow, Mistress, and dark is the
        night,
strange voices cry in the trees, intoning strange lore,
and more than cats move, lit by our eyes' green light,
on silent feet where the meadow grasses hang hoar –
Mistress, there are portents abroad of magic and might,
and things that are yet to be done. Open the door!

ELIZABETH COATSWORTH

A PATH TO THE MOON

From my front door there's a path to the moon
that nobody seems to see
tho it's marked with stones & grass & trees
there's nobody sees it but me.

You walk straight ahead for ten trees or so
turn left at the robin's song
follow the sound of the west wind down
past where the deer drink from the pond.

You take a right turn as the river bends
then where the clouds touch the earth
close your left eye & count up to ten
while twirling for all that you're worth.

And if you keep walking right straight ahead
clambering over the clouds
saying your mother's & father's names
over & over out loud

you'll come to the place where moonlight's born
the place where the moonbeams hide
and visit all of the crater sites
on the dark moon's secret side.

From my front door there's a path to the moon
that nobody seems to see
tho it's marked with stones & grass & trees
no one sees it but you & me.

b.p. NICHOL

BATS

A bat is born
Naked and blind and pale.
His mother makes a pocket of her tail
And catches him. He clings to her long fur
By his thumbs and toes and teeth.
And then the mother dances through the night
Doubling and looping, soaring, somersaulting –
Her baby hangs on underneath.
All night, in happiness, she hunts and flies.
Her high sharp cries
Like shining needlepoints of sound
Go out into the night and, echoing back,
Tell her what they have touched.
She hears how far it is, how big it is,
Which way it's going:
She lives by hearing.
The mother eats the moths and gnats she catches
In full flight; in full flight
The mother drinks the water of the pond
She skims across. Her baby hangs on tight.
Her baby drinks the milk she makes him
In moonlight or starlight, in mid-air.
Their single shadow, printed on the moon
Or fluttering across the stars,
Whirls on all night; at daybreak
The tired mother flaps home to her rafter.
The others all are there.
They hang themselves up by their toes,
They wrap themselves in their brown wings.
Bunched upside down, they sleep in air.

Their sharp ears, their sharp teeth, their quick sharp faces
Are dull and slow and mild.
All the bright day, as the mother sleeps,
She folds her wings about her sleeping child.

RANDALL JARRELL

FIRE BURN; AND CAULDRON, BUBBLE

Round about the cauldron go;
In the poison'd entrails throw.
Toad, that under cold stone
Days and nights has thirty-one
Swelter'd venom, sleeping got,
Boil thou first i'th'charmed pot.
Double, double toil and trouble:
Fire, burn; and cauldron, bubble.
Fillet of a fenny snake,
In the cauldron boil and bake;
Eye of newt, and toe of frog,
Wool of bat, and tongue of dog,
Adder's fork, and blind-worm's sting,
Lizard's leg, and howlet's wing,
For a charm of powerful trouble,
Like a hell-broth boil and bubble.
Double, double toil and trouble:
Fire burn; and cauldron, bubble.

WILLIAM SHAKESPEARE

APPLEMOON

Something woke me: startle-sound
or moonlight. The house dreamt
like an old cat, but I
looked out my window.

And night was day in a midnight
moon-flood. Mazy moon
flaring a halo of quick clouds
running the big black sky.
And I saw a thousand windfall apples
lying luminous as sea-stones beached
below the spiky silver trees.

So, shivering I
mouse-went out
with a basket, barefoot, toes
curling in the cold;
and singing soft
took ripe reluctant apples
under close and curious stars.

Only soon I saw
my shadow was not
the same as I;
it stooped more –
had its own thinness ...
and our fingers
never met.

I quick-ran back
the house so
sleepy-warm, sure.
But looking out through curtain lace
I saw my shadow linger
moving slow and crooked, plucking
shadow apples
from the shining moony grass.

ROSE FLINT

THE TWO RAVENS

There were two ravens who sat on a tree,
and they were black as they could be;
and one of them I heard him say,
Oh where shall we go to dine today?
Shall we go down to the salt, salt sea,
or shall we dine by the greenwood tree?

As I walked down on the white sea sand
I saw a fair ship sailing near at hand.
I waved my wings, I bent my beak,
that ship she sank and I heard a shriek.
There lie the sailors, one, two, and three.
Oh shall we go dine by the wild salt sea?

Come, I shall show you a far better sight –
a lonesome glen, and a new-slain knight:

his blood yet on the grass is hot,
his sword half-drawn, his shafts unshot.
And no one knows that he lies there
but his hound, his hawk, and his lady fair.

His hound is to the hunting gone,
his hawk to fetch the wild owl home,
his lady's gone to another mate.
Oh shall we make our feasting sweet!
Our dinner is sure, our feasting is free.
Oh come and we'll dine by the greenwood tree!

Oh you shall tear at his naked white thighs,
and I'll peck out his fair blue eyes.
You can pull a lock of his fine yellow hair
to thicken your nest where it grows bare.
The golden down on his young chin
will do to rest my young ones in.

Oh cold and bare will his bed be
when grey winter storms sing in the tree.
His head's on the turf, at his feet a stone –
He'll sleep nor hear young maidens mourn.
Over his white bones the birds will fly,
the wild deer run, the foxes cry.

TRADITIONAL

BLOW, BUGLE, BLOW

The splendour falls on castle walls
    And snowy summits old in story:
The long light shakes across the lakes,
    And the wild cataract leaps in glory.
Blow, bugle, blow, set the wild echoes flying,
Blow, bugle; answer, echoes, dying, dying, dying.

O hark, O hear! how thin and clear,
    And thinner, clearer, farther, going!
O sweet and far from cliff and scar
    The horns of Elfland faintly blowing!
Blow, let us hear the purple glens replying:
Blow, bugle; answer, echoes, dying, dying, dying.

O love, they die in yon rich sky,
    They faint on hill or field or river:
Our echoes roll from soul to soul,
    And grow for ever and for ever.
Blow, bugle, blow, set the wild echoes flying,
And answer, echoes, answer, dying, dying, dying.

ALFRED, LORD TENNYSON

SONG OF THE FISHING GHOSTS

Night is the time when phantoms play,
    Flows the river,
    Phantoms white
    Phantoms black
Fish in the dark salt water bay.

Skulls are nets for phantom fishers,
    Flows the river,
Phantoms red on a phantom river
    Dark flows the river.

Black phantom splashes,
    Flows the river,
White phantom splashes
    Flows the river.

Night is the time when phantoms play,
    Heads are nets
    For phantom fishers
There on the dark salt water bay.

Phantoms black
Phantoms red
Phantoms white
For nets their heads
And the dark, dark, dark river flows.

EFUA SUTHERLAND

GREEN MAN IN THE GARDEN

Green man in the garden
    Staring from the tree,
Why do you look so long and hard
    Through the pane at me?

Your eyes are dark as holly,
    Of sycamore your horns,
Your bones are made of elder-branch,
    Your teeth are made of thorns.

Your hat is made of ivy-leaf,
    Of bark your dancing shoes,
And evergreen and green and green
    Your jacket and shirt and trews.

Leave your house and leave your land
    And throw away the key,
And never look behind, he creaked,
    And come and live with me.

I bolted up the window,
    I bolted up the door,
I drew the blind that I should find
    The green man never more.

But when I softly turned the stair
    As I went up to bed,
I saw the green man standing there.
    Sleep well, my friend, he said.

EFUA SUTHERLAND

PRINCE KANO

In a dark wood Prince Kano lost his way
And searched in vain through the long summer's day.
At last, when night was near, he came in sight
Of a small clearing filled with yellow light,
And there, bending beside his brazier, stood
A charcoal burner wearing a black hood.
The Prince cried out for joy: 'Good friend, I'll give
What you will ask: guide me to where I live.'
The man pulled back his hood: he had no face –
Where it should be there was an empty space.

Half dead with fear the Prince staggered away,
Rushed blindly through the wood till break of day;
And then he saw a larger clearing, filled
With houses, people, but his soul was chilled;
He looked around for comfort, and his search
Led him inside a small, half-empty church
Where monks prayed. 'Father,' to one he said,
'I've seen a dreadful thing; I am afraid.'
'What did you see, my son?' 'I saw a man
Whose face was like ...' and, as the Prince began,
The monk drew back his hood and seemed to hiss,
Pointing to where his face should be, 'like this?'

EDWARD LOWBURY

THE KEY OF THE KINGDOM

This is the Key of the Kingdom:
In that Kingdom there is a city;
In that city is a town;
In that town there is a street;
In that street there winds a lane;
In that lane there is a yard;
In that yard there is a house;
In that house there waits a room;
In that room an empty bed;
And on that bed a basket –
A basket of sweet flowers:
Of flowers, of flowers;
A basket of sweet flowers.

Flowers in a basket;
Basket on the bed;
Bed in the chamber;
Chamber in the house;
House in the weedy yard;
Yard in the winding lane;
Lane in the broad street;
Street in the high town;
Town in the city;
City in the Kingdom –
This is the Key of the Kingdom.
Of the Kingdom this is the Key.

ANONYMOUS

THE CENTURION

'What is it now? More trouble?
Another Jew? I might have known it.
These Jews, they buzz around the tail of trouble
Like lascivious flies. Do they think we're here
Because we love them? Is it their climate
That holds us here? Why think, Marcellus –
By God, just dream of it. To-day in Rome,
Less than two thousand thirsty miles away,
Fountains and squares and shaded colonnades,
Men with smooth chins and girls that sometimes wash.
Well, who is it?   ... I see.
Another to be taken to that bonehill.
They're coming now. Just listen to them! –
You'd think they had a dozen there at least.
My sword, Marcellus, I'll be back to dinner.
Unless this fellow's a reluctant dier
Who loves the world too well.
Halt! Stop that shouting. Why is he dressed like that?
(His robes are purple. On his head
A hedge-crown. Where the thorns are driven
Berries of blood leap up ...) My Orders differ.
Remove that crown – at once – return his clothes.
Kingship can wait until his throne is ready.
Till then, safe conduct. Hold your lines –
Especially that to windward: I've no fondness
For foreign spittle. Hold them. March ...'
'Halt! Here's the place. Set down the cross.
You three attend to it. And remember, Marcus,
The blows are struck, the nails are driven

For Roman law and Roman order,
Not for your private satisfaction.
Set to work.'
(This grass is bare, sand-coloured: the hill
Quivers with heat.) 'What? As you please.
Seamless? – Then dice for it.' (The sun
Is brutal in this land, metallic.
It works for death, not life.) 'Well, is it done?
Now nail the board above: "King of the Jews."
That turns the mockery on them. Watch them wince
At the superscription. Look, their faces!
Hate, which man is hated most,
Myself or him? He'll serve for both:
They know their limitations. They know,
Greek, Jew or Roman, there is one command,
One only. What's his name –
He takes it quietly. From Nazareth?
I know it well. Who would exchange it
For this sad city, and become
The food for flies? Marcus there!
Give him some wine: he won't last long.'
That strain of wrist, the arms tension
And scarecrow hang of chest. 'Ah well,
Poor devil, he's got decent eyes.'

CLIVE SANSOM

THE JACKDAW OF RHEIMS

The Jackdaw sat on the Cardinal's chair!
Bishop and abbot and prior were there;
  Many a monk and many a friar,
  Many a knight and many a squire,
With a great many more of lesser degree, –
In sooth a goodly company;
And they served the Lord Primate on bended knee.
  Never I ween
  Was a prouder seen,
Read of in books, or dreamt of in dreams,
Than the Cardinal Lord Archbishop of Rheims!

  In and Out
  Through the motley rout,
That little Jackdaw kept hopping about;
  Here and there
  Like a dog in a fair,
  Over comfits and cates,
  And dishes and plates,
Cowl and cope, and rochet and pall,
Mitre and crosier! he hopp'd upon all!
  With saucy air,
  He perch'd on the chair
Where, in state, the great Lord Cardinal sat
In the great Lord Cardinal's great red hat.
  And he peer'd in the face
  Of his Lordship's Grace
With a satisfied look, as if he would say,
'We two are the greatest folks here to-day!'

And the priests, with awe,
As such freaks they saw,
Said, 'The Devil must be in that little Jackdaw!'

The feast was over. The board was clear'd.
The flawns and the custards had all disappear'd.
And six little singing boys, – dear little souls!
In nice clean faces, and nice white stoles,
  Came, in order due,
  Two by two,
Marching that grand refectory through!

A nice little boy held a golden ewer,
Emboss'd and fill'd with water, as pure
As any that flows between Rheims and Namur,
Which a nice little boy stood ready to catch
In a fine golden hand-basin made to match.
Two nice little boys, rather more grown,
Carried lavender-water, and eau de Cologne;
And a nice little boy had a nice cake of soap,
Worthy of washing the hands of the Pope.
  One little boy more
  A napkin bore
Of the best white diaper, fringed with pink,
And a Cardinal's Hat mark'd in permanent ink.
The great Lord Cardinal turns at the sight
Of these nice little boys dress'd all in white.
  From his finger he draws
  His costly turquoise;
And, not thinking at all about little Jackdaws,
  Deposits it straight

By the side of his plate,
While the nice little boys on his Eminence wait;
Till, when nobody's dreaming of any such thing,
That little Jackdaw hops off with the ring!

There's a cry and a shout,
And a deuce of a rout,
And nobody seems to know what they're about,
But the monks have their pockets all turn'd inside out.
The friars are kneeling,
And hunting, and feeling
The carpet, the floor, and the walls, and the ceiling.
The Cardinal drew
Off each plum-colour'd shoe,
And left his red stockings exposed to the view;
He peeps, and he feels
In the toes and the heels.
They turn up the dishes. They turn up the plates.
They take up the poker and poke out the grates.
They turn up the rugs.
They examine the mugs.
But, no! – no such thing; –
They can't find THE RING!
And the Abbot declared that, 'when nobody twigg'd it,
Some rascal or other had popp'd in, and prigg'd it!'

The Cardinal rose with a dignified look.
He call'd for his candle, his bell, and his book!
In holy anger and pious grief
He solemnly cursed that rascally thief!
He cursed him at board, he cursed him in bed,

From the sole of his foot to the crown of his head;
He cursed him in sleeping, that every night
He should dream of the devil, and wake in a fright;
He cursed him in eating, he cursed him in drinking,
He cursed him in coughing, in sneezing, in winking;
He cursed him in sitting, in standing, in lying;
He cursed him in walking, in riding, in flying,
He cursed him in living, he cursed him in dying! –
Never was heard such a terrible curse!
But what gave rise
To no little surprise –
Nobody seem'd one penny the worse!

The day was gone.
The night came on.
The Monks and the Friars they search'd till dawn,
When the Sacristan saw,
On crumpled claw,
Come limping a poor little lame Jackdaw!
No longer gay,
As on yesterday;
His feathers all seem'd to be turn'd the wrong way; –
His pinions droop'd – he could hardly stand, –
His head was as bald as the palm of your hand;
His eyes so dim,
So wasted each limb,
That, heedless of grammar, they all cried, 'THAT'S HIM! –
That's the scamp that has done this scandalous thing!
That's the thief that has got my Lord Cardinal's Ring!'

The poor little Jackdaw,
  When the Monks he saw,
Feebly gave vent to the ghost of a caw;
And turn'd his bald head, as much as to say,
'Pray, be so good as to walk this way!'
  Slower and slower
  He limp'd on before,
Till they came to the back of the belfry door,
  Where the first thing they saw,
  Midst the sticks and the straw,
Was the RING in the nest of that little Jackdaw!

Then the great Lord Cardinal call'd for his book
And off that terrible curse he took.
  The mute expression
  Served in lieu of confession,
And, being thus coupled with full restitution,
The Jackdaw got plenary absolution!
  –When those words were heard,
    That poor little bird
Was so changed in a moment, 'twas really absurd.
  He grew sleek, and fat.
  In addition to that,
A fresh crop of feathers came thick as a mat!

  His tail waggled more
  Even than before.
But no longer it wagg'd with an impudent air.
No longer he perch'd on the Cardinal's chair.
  He hopp'd now about
  With a gait devout.

At Matins, at Vespers, he never was out.
And, so far from any more pilfering deeds,
He always seem'd telling the Confessor's beads.
If any one lied, – or if any one swore, –
Or slumber'd in prayer-time and happen'd to snore,
  That good Jackdaw
  Would give a great 'Caw!'
As much as to say, 'Don't do so any more!'
While many remark'd, as his manners they saw,
That they 'never had known such a pious Jackdaw!'
  He long lived the pride
  Of that country-side,
And at last in the odour of sanctity died;
  When, as words were too faint
  His merits to paint,
The Conclave determined to make him a Saint;
And on newly made Saints and Popes, as you know,
It's the custom, at Rome, new names to bestow,
So they canonized him by the name of 'Jim Crow'!

RICHARD HARRIS BARHAM

THE SYCOPHANTIC FOX AND THE GULLIBLE RAVEN

A raven sat upon a tree,
    And not a word he spoke, for
His beak contained a piece of Brie,
    Or, maybe, it was Roquefort?
        We'll make it any kind you please –
        At all events, it was a cheese.

Beneath the tree's umbrageous limb
    A hungry fox sat smiling;
He saw the raven watching him,
    And spoke in words beguiling:
        'J'admire,' said he, 'ton beau plumage.'
        (The which was simply persiflage.)

Two things there are, no doubt you know,
    To which a fox is used –
A rooster that is bound to crow,
    A crow that's bound to roost,
        And whichsoever he espies
        He tells the most unblushing lies.

'Sweet fowl,' he said, 'I understand
    You're more than merely natty:
I hear you sing to beat the band
    And Adelina Patti.
        Pray render with your liquid tongue
        A bit from *Götterdämmerung*.'

This subtle speech was aimed to please
    The crow, and it succeeded:
He thought no bird in all the trees
    Could sing as well as he did.
        In flattery completely doused
        He gave the 'Jewel Song' from *Faust*.

But gravitation's law, of course,
    As Isaac Newton showed it,
Exerted on the cheese its force,
    And elsewhere soon bestowed it.
        In fact, there is no need to tell
        What happened when to earth it fell.

I blush to add that when the bird
    Took in the situation,
He said one brief, emphatic word,
    Unfit for publication.
        The fox was greatly startled, but
        He only sighed and answered 'Tut!'

THE MORAL IS: A fox is bound
    To be a shameless sinner.
And also: When the cheese comes round
    You know it's after dinner.
        But (what is only known to few)
        The fox is after dinner, too.

GUY WETMORE CARRYL

THE CROWN OF ROSES

When Jesus Christ was yet a child
He had a garden small and wild,
Wherein he cherished roses fair
And wove them into garlands there.

Now once as summer time drew nigh
There came a troop of children by,
And seeing roses on a tree,
With shouts they plucked them merrily.

'Do you bind roses in your hair?'
They cried in scorn to Jesus there.
The boy said humbly, 'Take I pray
All but the naked thorns away.'

Then of the thorns they made a crown,
And with rough fingers pressed it down,
Till on his forehead fair and young
Red drops of blood like roses sprung.

RUSSIAN CAROL

IN THE SERVANTS' QUARTERS

'Man, you too, aren't you, one of these rough followers of the
    criminal?
All hanging hereabouts to gather how he's going to bear
Examination in the hall.' She flung disdainful glances on
The shabby figure standing at the fire with others there,
    Who warmed them by its flare.

'No indeed, my skipping maiden: I know nothing of the trial here,
Or criminal, if so he be. – I chanced to come this way,
And the fire shone out into the dawn, and morning airs are cold now;
I, too, was drawn in part by charms I see before me play,
    That I see not every day.'

'Ha, ha!' then laughed the constables who also stood to warm themselves,
The while another maiden scrutinized his features hard,
As the blaze threw into contrast every line and knot that wrinkled them,
Exclaiming, 'Why, last night when he was brought in by the guard,
    You were with him in the yard!'

'Nay, nay, you teasing wench, I say! You know you speak mistakenly.
Cannot a tired pedestrian who has legged it long and far
Here on his way from northern parts, engrossed in humble marketings,
Come in and rest awhile, although judicial doings are
    Afoot by morning star?'
'O, come, come!' laughed the constables. 'Why, man, you speak the dialect
He uses in his answers; you can hear him up the stairs.
So own it. We sha'n't hurt ye. There he's speaking now! His syllables
Are those you sound yourself when you are talking unawares,
    As this pretty girl declares.'

'And you shudder when his chain clinks!' she rejoined. 'O yes, I noticed it.
And you winced, too, when those cuffs they gave him echoed to us here.
They'll soon be coming down, and you may then have to defend yourself
Unless you hold your tongue, or go away and keep you clear
    When he's led to judgment near!'

'No! I'll be damned in hell if I know anything about the man!
No single thing about him more than everybody knows!
Must not I even warm my hands but I am charged with blasphemies?' ...
– His face convulses as the morning cock that moment crows,
    And he droops, and turns, and goes.

THOMAS HARDY

BALLAD OF THE BREAD MAN

Mary stood in the kitchen
    Baking a loaf of bread.
An angel flew in through the window.
    'We've a job for you,' he said.

'God in his big gold heaven,
    Sitting in his big blue chair,
Wanted a mother for his little son.
    Suddenly saw you there.'

Mary shook and trembled,
    'It isn't true what you say.'
'Don't say that,' said the angel.
    'The baby's on its way.'

Joseph was in the workshop
    Planing a piece of wood.
'The old man's past it,' the neighbours said.
    'That girl's been up to no good.'

'And who was that elegant fellow,'
    They said, 'in the shiny gear?'
The things they said about Gabriel
    Were hardly fit to hear.

Mary never answered,
    Mary never replied.
She kept the information,
    Like the baby, safe inside.

It was election winter.
  They went to vote in town.
When Mary found her time had come
  The hotels let her down.

The baby was born in an annexe
  Next to the local pub.
At midnight, a delegation
  Turned up from the Farmers' Club.

They talked about an explosion
  That made a hole in the sky,
Said they'd been sent to the Lamb & Flag
  To see God come down from on high.

A few days later a bishop
  And a five-star general were seen
With the head of an African country
  In a bullet-proof limousine.

'We've come,' they said, 'with tokens
  For the little boy to choose.'
Told the tale about war and peace
  In the television news.

After them came the soldiers
  With rifle and bomb and gun,
Looking for enemies of the state.
  The family had packed and gone.

When they got back to the village
    The neighbours said, to a man,
'That boy will never be one of us,
    Though he does what he blessed well can.'

He went round to all the people
    A paper crown on his head.
Here is some bread from my father.
    Take, eat, he said.

Nobody seemed very hungry.
    Nobody seemed to care.
Nobody saw the god in himself
    Quietly standing there.

He finished up in the papers.
    He came to a very bad end.
He was charged with bringing the living to life.
    No man was that prisoner's friend.

There's only one kind of punishment
    To fit that kind of crime.
They rigged a trial and shot him dead.
    They were only just in time.

They lifted the young man by the leg,
    They lifted him by the arm,
They locked him in a cathedral
    In case he came to harm.

They stored him safe as water
    Under seven rocks.
One Sunday morning he burst out
    Like a jack-in-the-box.

Through the town he went walking.
    He showed them the holes in his head.
Now do you want any loaves? he cried.
    'Not today,' they said.

CHARLES CAUSLEY

WHAT THE DONKEY SAW

No room in the inn, of course,
And not that much in the stable,
What with the shepherds, Magi, Mary,
Joseph, the heavenly host –
Not to mention the baby
Using our manger as a cot.
You couldn't have squeezed another cherub in
For love or money.

Still, in spite of the overcrowding,
I did my best to make them feel wanted.
I could see the baby and I
Would be going places together.

U.A. FANTHORPE

ANIMAL RIGHTS

Our cat
Won't use the cat-flap
Any more.
He's started to fight
For his Animal Rights
And insists
That he uses the door.

LINDSAY MacRAE

PETS

A dark November night, late. The back door wide.
Beyond the doorway, the step off into space.
On the threshold, looking out,
With foxy-furry tail lifted, a kitten.
Somewhere out there, a badger, our lodger,
A stripe-faced rusher at cats, a grim savager,
Is crunching the bones and meat of a hare
Left out for her nightly emergence
From under the outhouses.

The kitten flirts his tail, arches his back –
All his hairs are inquisitive.
Dare he go for a pee?
Something is moving there, just in dark.
A prowling lump. A tabby tom. Grows.
And the battered master of the house
After a month at sea, comes through the doorway,

Recovered from his nearly fatal mauling,
Two probably three pounds heavier
Since that last time he dragged in for help.
He deigns to recognize me
With his criminal eyes, his deformed voice.
Then poises, head lowered, muscle-bound,
Like a bull for the judges,
A thick Devon bull,
Sniffing the celebration of sardines.

TED HUGHES

AN OLD CAT'S CONFESSIONS

I am a very old pussy,
My name is Tabitha Jane;
I have had about fifty kittens,
So I think that I mustn't complain.

Yet I've had my full share of cat's troubles:
I was run over once by a cart;
And they drowned seventeen of my babies,
Which came near breaking my heart.

A gentleman once singed my whiskers, –
I shall never forgive him for that!
And once I was bit by a mad dog,
And once was deceived by a rat.

I was tied by some boys in a meal-bag,
And pelted and pounded with stones;
They thought I was mashed to a jelly,
But it didn't break one of my bones.

For cats that have good constitutions
Have eight more lives than a man;
Which proves we are better than humans
To my mind, if anything can.

One night, as I wandered with Thomas, –
We were singing a lovely duet, –
I was shot in the back by a bullet;
When you stroke me, I feel it there yet.

A terrior once threatened my kittens;
    O, it gave me a terrible fright!
But I scratched him, and sent him off howling
    And I think that I served him just right.

But I've failed to fulfil all my duties:
    I have purred half my life in a dream;
And I never devoured the canary,
    And I never lapped half enough cream.

But I've been a pretty good mouser,
    (What squirrels and birds I have caught)
And have brought up my frolicsome kittens
    As a dutiful mother-cat ought.

Now I think I've a right, being aged,
    To take an old tabby's repose;
To have a good breakfast and dinner,
    And sit by the fire and doze.

I don't care much for the people
    Who are living with me in this house,
But I own that I love a good fire,
    And occasional herring and mouse.

C. P. CRANCH

AH, ARE YOU DIGGING ON MY GRAVE?

'Ah, are you digging on my grave,
      My loved one? – planting rue?'
– 'No: yesterday he went to wed
One of the brightest wealth has bred.
"It cannot hurt her now," he said,
      "that I should not be true."'

'Then who is digging on my grave?
      My nearest dearest kin?'
– 'Ah, no: they sit and think, "What use!
What good will planting flowers produce?
No tendance of her mound can loose
      Her spirit from Death's gin."'

'But some one digs upon my grave?
      My enemy? – prodding sly?'
– 'Nay: when she heard you had passed the Gate
That shuts on all flesh soon or late,
She thought you no more worth her hate,
      And cares not where you lie.'

'Then, who is digging on my grave?
      Say – since I have not guessed!'
– 'O it is I, my mistress dear,
Your little dog, who still lives near,
And much I hope my movements here
      Have not disturbed your rest?'

'Ah, yes! *You* dig upon my grave ....
    Why flashed it not on me
That one true heart was left behind!
What feeling do we ever find
To equal among human kind
    A dog's fidelity!'

'Mistress, I dug upon your grave
    To bury a bone, in case
I should be hungry near this spot
When passing on my daily trot.
I am sorry, but I quite forgot
    It was your resting-place.'

THOMAS HARDY

I SAW

I saw a peacock with a fiery tail
I saw a blazing comet drop down hail
I saw a cloud with ivy circled round
I saw a sturdy oak creep on the ground
I saw an ant swallow up a whale
I saw a raging sea brim full of ale
I saw a Venice glass sixteen foot deep
I saw a well full of men's tears that weep
I saw their eyes all in a flame of fire
I saw a house as big as the moon and higher
I saw the sun even in the midst of night
I saw the man that saw this wondrous sight.

I saw a fishpond all on fire
I saw a house bow to a squire
I saw a parson twelve feet high
I saw a cottage near the sky
I saw a balloon made of lead
I saw a coffin drop down dead
I saw a sparrow run a race
I saw two horses making lace
I saw a girl just like a cat
I saw a kitten wear a hat
I saw a man who saw these too,
And says, though strange, they all are true.

ANONYMOUS

CAT WARMTH

All afternoon,
My cat sleeps,
On the end of my bed.

When I creep my toes
Down between the cold sheets,
I find a patch of cat-warmth
That he's left behind;
An invisible gift.

JOHN CUNLIFFE

THE OWL AND THE PUSSY-CAT

The Owl and the Pussy-Cat went to sea
    In a beautiful pea-green boat.
They took some honey, and plenty of money,
    Wrapped up in a five-pound note.
The Owl looked up to the stars above,
    And sang to a small guitar,
'O lovely Pussy! O Pussy, my love,
    What a beautiful Pussy you are,
        You are,
        You are!
    What a beautiful Pussy you are!'

Pussy said to the Owl, 'You elegant fowl!
    How charmingly sweet you sing!
O let us be married! too long we have tarried:
    But what shall we do for a ring?'
They sailed away, for a year and a day,
    To the land where the Bong-Tree grows,
And there in a wood a Piggy-wig stood,
    With a ring at the end of his nose,
        His nose,
        His nose,
    With a ring at the end of his nose.

'Dear Pig, are you willing to sell for one shilling
    Your ring?' Said the Piggy, 'I will.'
So they took it away, and were married next day
    By the Turkey who lives on the hill.
They dined on mince, and slices of quince,
    Which they ate with a runcible spoon;
And hand in hand, on the edge of the sand,
    They danced by the light of the moon,
        The moon,
        The moon,
    They danced by the light of the moon.

EDWARD LEAR

IT'S A DOG'S LIFE

Mum says
Our dog's
Having an identity crisis.

Yesterday,
He went out into the garden,
Then tried to come back in
Through the cat-flap.

He jammed his head so tight,
No matter how hard
We pushed and pulled
It wouldn't budge.

In the end,
We had to call the fire brigade.

When Dad came home
He nearly had a fit,
When he saw
What they'd done to the door.

He called the dog
All sorts of names.
But when the dog jumped up
To beg for his evening walk,
Dad still took him.

It's not fair.
If I'd smashed the door,
I wouldn't have been allowed out
For at least two weeks!

JOHN FOSTER

DISABLED

He sat in a wheeled chair, waiting for dark,
And shivered in his ghastly suit of grey,
Legless, sewn short at elbow. Through the park
Voices of boys rang saddening like a hymn,
Voices of play and pleasure after day,
Till gathering sleep had mothered them from him.

About this time Town used to swing so gay
When glow-lamps budded in the light blue trees,
And girls glanced lovelier as the air grew dim, –
In the old times, before he threw away his knees.
Now he will never feel again how slim
Girls' waists are, or how warm their subtle hands;
All of them touch him like some queer disease.

There was an artist silly for his face,
For it was younger than his youth, last year.
Now, he is old; his back will never brace;
He's lost his colour very far from here,
Poured it down shell-holes till the veins ran dry,
And half his lifetime lapsed in the hot race
And leap of purple spurted from his thigh.
One time he liked a blood-smear down his leg,
After the matches, carried shoulder-high.
It was after football, when he'd drunk a peg,
He thought he'd better join. – He wonders why.
Someone had said he'd look a god in kilts,
That's why; and maybe, too, to please his Meg;
Aye, that was it, to please the giddy jilts

He asked to join. He didn't have to beg;
Smiling they wrote his lie; aged nineteen years.
Germans he scarcely thought of; all their guilt
And Austria's, did not move him. And no fears
Of Fear came yet. He thought of jewelled hilts
For daggers in plaid socks; of smart salutes;
And care of arms; and leave; and pay arrears;
Esprit de corps; and hints for young recruits.
And soon, he was drafted out with drums and cheers.

Some cheered him home, but not as crowds cheer Goal.
Only a solemn man who brought him fruits
Thanked him; and then inquired about his soul.
Now, he will spend a few sick years in institutes,
And do what things the rules consider wise,
And take whatever pity they may dole.
Tonight he noticed how the women's eyes
Passed from him to the strong men that were whole.
How cold and late it is! Why don't they come
And put him into bed? Why don't they come?

WILFRED OWEN

MILITARY CEMETERY

Such discipline on parade
Would put to shame a Guards' Brigade;
So long, so rigid, to remain like this
And still no order to dismiss.

WILLIAM CLARKE

DEAD GERMAN YOUTH

He lay there, mutilated and forlorn,
Save that his face was woundless, and his hair
Drooped forward and caressed his boyish brow.
He looked so tired, as if his life had been
Too full of pain and anguish to endure,
And like a weary child who tires of play
He lay there, waiting for decay.
I feel no anger towards you, German boy,
Whom war has driven down the path of pain.
Would God we could have met in peace
And laughed and talked with tankards full of beer,
For I would rather hear your youthful mirth
At stories which I often loved to tell
Than stand here looking down at you
So terrible, so quiet and so still.

C.P.S. DENHOLM-YOUNG

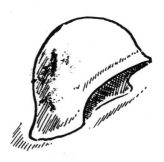

POINT OF VIEW
(HEARD IN A BUTCHER'S SHOP, BOLTON, LANCS)

'It's slaughter – nothing more nor less –
The bombing in this war ...
A dreadful thing ... you'd never guess
The shocking sights we saw
In London, when the Blitz was on ...
A leg hung from a tree;
A body with the top half gone
And nowt below the knee;
A hand with wedding ring and all;
Two feet in socks and boots;
A baby's head stuck to a shawl;
An arm torn by the roots;
While here and there was flesh in lumps
They shovelled into sacks.
It proper left us in the dumps ...
Sent shivers down our backs.'

'It's slaughter, sir. I've seen a bit
Of what those swine can do.'
His chopper fell and fiercely split
A sheep's head clean in two.
'It's downright murder to attack
Defenceless folk who can't fight back!'
... And swinging dumbly on a hook,
A dead pig gave him such a look.

R. P. BRETT

SALVAGE SONG (OR: THE HOUSEWIFE'S DREAM)

My saucepans have all been surrendered,
The teapot is gone from the hob,
The colander's leaving the cabbage
For a very much different job.
So now, when I hear on the wireless
Of Hurricanes showing their mettle,
I see, in a vision before me,
A Dornier chased by my kettle.

ELSIE CAWSER

AN AUSTRIAN ARMY

An Austrian army awfully array'd
Boldly by battery besieged Belgrade.
Cossack commanders cannonading come
Dealing destruction's devastating doom:
Every endeavour engineers essay,
For fame, for fortune fighting-furious fray!
Generals 'gainst generals grapple, gracious God!
How Heaven honours heroic hardihood!
Infuriate – indiscriminate in ill –
Kinsmen kill kindred – kindred kinsmen kill:
Labour low levels loftiest, longest lines,
Men march 'mid moles, 'mid murd'rous
      mines:
Now noisy noxious numbers notice nought
Of outward obstacles, opposing ought –
Poor patriots – partly purchased – partly press'd
Quite quaking, quickly 'Quarter! quarter!' quest:
Reason returns, religious right redounds,
Suwarrow stops such sanguinary sounds.
Truce to thee, Turkey, triumph to thy train,
Unwise, unjust, unmerciful Ukraine!
Vanish, vain victory! Vanish, victory vain!
Why wish we warfare? Wherefore welcome were
Xerxes, Ximenes, Xanthus, Xavier?
Yield, yield, ye youths, ye yeomen, yield your yell:
Zeno's, Zimmermann's, Zoroaster's zeal,
Again attract; arts against arms appeal!

ALARIC A. WATTS

LONDON BELLS

Gay go up, and gay go down
To ring the bells of London town.

Bull's eyes and targets,
Say the bells of St Marg'ret's.

Brickbats and tiles,
Say the bells of St Giles'.

Oranges and lemons,
Say the bells of St Clement's.

Pancakes and fritters,
Say the bells of St Peter's.

Two sticks and an apple,
Say the bells at Whitechapel.

Old Father Baldpate,
Say the slow bells at Aldgate.

Maids in white aprons,
Say the bells of St Cath'rine's.

Pokers and tongs,
Say the bells at St John's.

Kettles and pans,
Say the bells at St Anne's.

You owe me ten shillings,
Say the bells at St Helen's.

When will you pay me?
Say the bells at Old Bailey.

When I grow rich,
Say the bells at Fleetditch.

When will that be?
Say the bells at Stepney.

I'm sure I don't know,
Says the great bell at Bow.

When I am old,
Say the bells at St Paul's.

Here comes a candle to light you to bed,
And here comes a chopper to chop off your head.

ANONYMOUS

THE DUEL

The gingham dog and the calico cat
Side by side on the table sat;
'Twas half-past twelve, and (what do you think!)
Nor one nor t'other had slept a wink!
    The old Dutch clock and the Chinese plate
    Appeared to know as sure as fate
There was going to be a terrible spat.
    (I wasn't there; I simply state
    What was told to me by the Chinese plate!)

The gingham dog went 'bow-wow-wow!'
And the calico cat replied 'mee-ow!'
The air was littered, an hour or so,
With bits of gingham and calico,
    While the old Dutch clock in the chimney-place
    Up with its hands before its face,
For it always dreaded a family row!
    (Now mind: I'm only telling you
    What the old Dutch clock declares is true!)

The Chinese plate looked very blue,
And wailed, 'Oh, dear! what shall we do!'
But the gingham dog and the calico cat
Wallowed this way and tumbled that,
    Employing every tooth and claw
    In the awfullest way you ever saw –
And, oh! how the gingham and calico flew!
    (Don't fancy I exaggerate –
    I got my news from the Chinese plate!)

Next morning, where the two had sat
They found no trace of dog or cat;
And some folks think unto this day
That burglars stole that pair away!
    But the truth about the cat and pup
    Is this: they ate each other up!
Now what do you really think of that!
    (The old Dutch clock it told me so,
    And that is how I came to know.)

EUGENE FIELD

COMBINATIONS

A flea flew by a bee. The bee
To flee the flea flew by a fly.
The fly flew high to flee the bee
Who flew to flee the flea who flew
To flee the fly who now flew by.

The bee flew by the fly. The fly
To flee the bee flew by the flea.
The flea flew high to flee the fly
Who flew to flee the bee who flew
To flee the flea who now flew by.

The fly flew by the flea. The flea
To flee the fly flew by the bee.
The bee flew high to flee the flea
Who flew to flee the fly who flew
To flee the bee who now flew by.

The flea flew by the fly. The fly
To flee the flea flew by the bee.
The bee flew high to flee the fly
Who flew to flee the flea who flew
To flee the bee who now flew by.

The fly flew by the bee. The bee
To flee the fly flew by the flea.
The flea flew high to flee the bee
Who flew to flee the fly who flew
To flee the flea who now flew by.

The bee flew by the flea. The flea
To flee the bee flew by the fly.
The fly flew high to flee the flea
Who flew to flee the bee who flew
To flee the fly who now flew by.

MARY ANN HOBERMAN

ABOU BEN ADHEM

Abou Ben Adhem (may his tribe increase!)
Awoke one night from a deep dream of peace,
And saw, within the moonlight in his room,
Making it rich, and like a lily in bloom,
An angel writing in a book of gold: –
Exceeding peace had made Ben Adhem bold,
And to the presence in the room he said,
'What writest thou?' The vision raised its head,
And with a look made of all sweet accord,
Answered, 'The names of those who love the Lord.'
'And is mine one?' said Abou. 'Nay, not so,'
Replied the angel. Abou spoke more low,
But cheerly still; and said, 'I pray thee, then,
Write me as one that loves his fellow men.'
The angel wrote, and vanished. The next night
It came again with a great wakening light,
And showed the names whom love of God had blest,
And lo! Ben Adhem's name led all the rest.

LEIGH HUNT

THE KING OF CATS SENDS A POSTCARD TO HIS WIFE

Keep your whiskers crisp and clean.
Do not let the mice grow lean.
Do not let yourself grow fat
like a common kitchen cat.

Have you set the kittens free?
Do they sometimes ask for me?
Is our catnip growing tall?
Did you patch the garden wall?

Clouds are gentle walls that hide
gardens on the other side.
Tell the tabby cats I take
all my meals with William Blake,

lunch at noon and tea at four,
served in splendour on the shore
at the tinkling of a bell.
Tell them I am sleeping well.

Tell them I have come so far,
brought by Blake's celestial car,
buffeted by wind and rain,
I may not get home again.

Take this message to my friends.
Say the King of Catnip sends
to the cat who winds his clocks
a thousand sunsets in a box,

to the cat who brings the ice
the shadows of a dozen mice
(serve them with assorted dips
and eat them like potato chips),

and to the cat who guards his door
a net for catching stars, and more
(if with patience he abide):
catnip from the other side.

NANCY WILLARD

FORTUNES

One for sorrow, two for joy,
Three for a kiss and four for a boy,
Five for silver, six for gold,
Seven for a secret never to be told,
Eight for a letter over the sea,
Nine for a lover as true as can be.

TRADITIONAL

THE LAMBS OF GRASMERE

The upland flocks grew starved and thinned:
    Their shepherds scarce could feed the lambs
Whose milkless mothers butted them,
    Or who were orphaned of their dams.
The lambs athirst for mother's milk
    Filled all the place with piteous sounds:
Their mothers' bones made white for miles
    The pastureless wet pasture grounds.

Day after day, night after night,
    From lamb to lamb the shepherds went,
With teapots for the bleating mouths,
    Instead of nature's nourishment.
The little shivering gaping things
    Soon knew the step that brought them aid,
And fondled the protecting hand,
    And rubbed it with a woolly head.

Then, as the days waxed on to weeks,
  It was a pretty sight to see
These lambs with frisky heads and tails
  Skipping and leaping on the lea,
Bleating in tender, trustful tones,
  Resting on rocky crag or mound,
And following the beloved feet
  That once had sought for them and found.

These very shepherds of their flocks,
  These loving lambs so meek to please,
Are worthy of recording words
  And honour in their due degrees:
So I might live a hundred years,
  And roam from strand to foreign strand,
Yet not forget this flooded spring
  And scarce-saved lambs of Westmoreland.

CHRISTINA ROSSETTI

SOMEWHERE AROUND CHRISTMAS

Always, or nearly always, on old apple trees,
Somewhere around Christmas, if you look up through the frost,
You will see, fat as a bullfinch, stuck on a high branch,
One lingering, bald, self-sufficient, hard, blunt fruit.

There will be no leaves, you can be sure of that;
The twigs will be tar-black, and the white sky
Will be grabbed among the branches like thumbed glass
In broken triangles just saved from crashing to the ground.

Further up, dribbles of rain will run down
Like spilt colourless varnish on a canvas. The old tins,
Tyres, cardboard boxes, debris of back gardens,
Will lie around, bleak, with mould and rust creeping over them.

Blow on your fingers. Wipe your feet on the mat by the back
    door.
You will never see that apple fall. Look at the cat,
Her whiskers twitch as she sleeps by the kitchen fire;
In her backyard prowling dream she thinks it's a bird.

JOHN SMITH

A BALLAD OF JOHN SILVER

We were schooner-rigged and rakish, with a long and lissome
    hull,
And we flew the pretty colours of the cross-bones and the skull;
We'd a big black Jolly Roger flapping grimly at the fore,
And we sailed the Spanish Water in the happy days of yore.

We'd a long brass gun amidships, like a well-conducted ship,
We had each a brace of pistols and a cutlass at the hip;
It's a point which tells against us, and a fact to be deplored,
But we chased the goodly merchant-men and laid their ships
    aboard.

Then the dead men fouled the scuppers and the wounded filled
    the chains,
And the paint-work all was spatter-dashed with other people's
    brains,
She was boarded, she was looted, she was scuttled till she sank,
And the pale survivors left us by the medium of the plank.

O! then it was (while standing by the taffrail on the poop)
We could hear the drowning folk lament the absent chicken-
    coop;
Then, having washed the blood away, we'd little else to do
Than to dance a quiet hornpipe as the old salts taught us to.

O! the fiddle on the fo'c'sle, and the slapping naked soles,
And the genial 'Down the middle, Jake, and curtsey when she
    rolls!'
When the silver seas around us and the pale moon overhead,

And the look-out Nat a-looking and his pipe-bowl glowing
    red.

Ah! the pig-tailed, quidding pirates and the pretty pranks we
    played,
All have since been put a stop-to by the naughty Board of Trade;
The schooners and the merry crews are laid away to rest,
A little south the sunset in the Islands of the Blest.

JOHN MASEFIELD

SCOTLAND SMALL?

Scotland small? Our multiform, our infinite Scotland small?
Only as a patch of hillside may be a cliché corner
To a fool who cries 'Nothing but heather!' Where in September
    another
Sitting there and resting and gazing round
Sees not only heather but blaeberries
With bright green leaves and leaves already turned scarlet,
Hiding ripe blue berries; and amongst the sage-green leaves
Of the bog-myrtle the golden flowers of the tormentil shining;
And on the small bare places, where the little Blackface sheep
Found grazing, milkworts blue as summer skies;
And down in neglected peat-hags, not worked
In living memory, sphagnum moss in pastel shades
Of yellow, green, and pink; sundew and butterwort
And nodding harebells vying in their colour
With the blue butterflies that poise themselves delicately upon
    them.
And stunted rowans with harsh dry leaves of glorious colour
'Nothing but heather!' – How marvellously descriptive! And
    incomplete!

HUGH MacDIARMID

RHINOCEROS

God simply got bored and started doodling
with ideas he'd given up on, scooping off the floor
bits and bobs and sticking them together,
the tail of a ten-ton pig he'd meant for Norway,
the long skull of a too-heavy dinosaur,
the armour plating of his first version of
the hippo; an unpainted beak of a toucan
stuck on back to front, a dash of tantrums
he intended for the Abyssinian owl, the same
awful grey colour he'd used for landscaping the moon.

And tempted to try it with the batteries,
he set it down on the wild plains of Africa,
grinned at what he saw and let it run.

MATT SIMPSON

THE BLUE ROOM

My room is blue, the carpet's blue,
The chairs are blue, the door's blue too.
A blue bird flew in yesterday,
I don't know if it's flown away.

RICHARD EDWARDS

THE DONKEY'S CHRISTMAS

Plodding on,
From inn to inn,
No room to spare,
No room but a stable bare.
We rest,
And the following morning Jesus is born.
I gaze on the wondrous sight.
The King is born,
The King in a stable.
I see great lights,
Lights that are angels.
Everyone comes to see this sight.
I carried Mary,
Holy Mary,
Last night.

ANONYMOUS

EXCELSIOR

The shades of night were falling fast,
As through an Alpine village passed
A youth, who bore, 'mid snow and ice,
A banner with the strange device,
  Excelsior!

His brow was sad; his eye beneath
Flashed like a falchion from its sheath,
And like a silver clarion rung
The accents of that unknown tongue,
  Excelsior!

In happy homes he saw the light
Of household fires gleam warm and bright;
Above, the spectral glaciers shone,
And from his lips escaped a groan,
  Excelsior!

'Try not the Pass!' the old man said,
'Dark lowers the tempest overhead,
The roaring torrent is deep and wide!'
And loud that clarion voice replied,
  Excelsior!

'O stay!' the maiden said, 'and rest
Thy weary head upon this breast!'
A tear stood in his bright blue eye,
But still he answered, with a sigh,
  Excelsior!

'Beware the pine-tree's withered branch!
Beware the awful avalanche!'
This was the peasant's last goodnight!
A voice replied, far up the height,
  Excelsior!

At break of day, as heavenward
The pious monks of Saint Bernard
Uttered the oft-repeated prayer,
A voice cried through the startled air,
  Excelsior!

A traveller, by the faithful hound,
Half-buried in the snow, was found,
Still grasping in his hand of ice
That banner, with the strange device
  Excelsior!

There, in the twilight cold and grey,
Lifeless, but beautiful, he lay,
And from the sky, serene, and far,
A voice fell, like a falling star,
  Excelsior!

HENRY WADSWORTH LONGFELLOW

BRITISH RAIL REGRETS

British Rail regrets
having to regret.
British Rail regrets
it cannot spell.
British Rail regrets
the chalk ran out.
British Rail regrets
that due to a staff shortage
there will be no one
to offer regrets.
British Rail regrets
but will not be sending
flowers or tributes.
British Rail regrets
the early arrival
of your train.
This was due to industrious action.
British Rail regrets
that because of a work-to-rule
by our tape machine
this is a real person.
British Rail regrets
the cheese shortage
in your sandwich.
This is due to
a points failure.
The steward got
three out of ten.

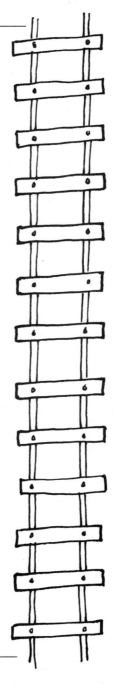

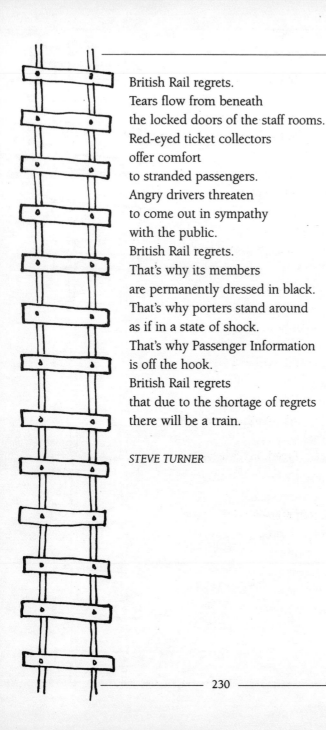

British Rail regrets.
Tears flow from beneath
the locked doors of the staff rooms.
Red-eyed ticket collectors
offer comfort
to stranded passengers.
Angry drivers threaten
to come out in sympathy
with the public.
British Rail regrets.
That's why its members
are permanently dressed in black.
That's why porters stand around
as if in a state of shock.
That's why Passenger Information
is off the hook.
British Rail regrets
that due to the shortage of regrets
there will be a train.

STEVE TURNER

MAMA DOT I

Born on a Sunday
in the kingdom of Ashante

Sold on Monday
into slavery

Ran away on Tuesday
cause she born free

Lost a foot on Wednesday
when they catch she

Worked all Thursday
till her head grey

Dropped on Friday
where they burned she

Freed on Saturday
in a new century

FRED D'AGUIAR

THE PANTOMIME

I remember the zip just
Wouldn't do up quickly enough,
As I pulled on my hand-me-down
Anorak. We were going to see
The Debenham Players!

I stumbled along
The darkened aisle, feeling like
The 'It' in Blind Man's Buff.
We waited, staring at
The silhouetted castle.
Then the curtain rose
And there she was!
Her stagnant-green hair
Protruded from the large black hat,
Planted firmly on her ugly head.
A large boil erupted
From her wrinkled nose.
And tongues of fire seemed to leap
From her finger-tips
As the spotlight flickered
On her witch's claws.
Her scream revealed
A scrap-heap of teeth.
Her piercing eyes had even the boldest
Of the audience silent.

As we filed out of the doors,
I peered around a screen.
There stood an actor;
He was robed in black
And wore a cheap green wig;
Orange plastic nails were sellotaped
To his fingers and he wore
Too much powder on his nose.

'That's funny,' I remember thinking,
'He wasn't in the show.'

TIM CONNORS

DAVID AND GOLIATH

Goliath of Gath
With hith helmet of brath
Wath theated one day
Upon the green grath.

When up thkipped thlim David
A thervant of Thaul,
And thaid I will thmite thee
Although I am tho thmall.

Thlim David thkipped down
To the edge of the thtream,
And from it'th thmooth thurface
Five thmooth thtones he took.

He loothened hith corthetth
And thevered hith head,
And all Ithrael thouted –
'Goliath ith dead!'

ANONYMOUS

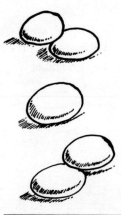

UPON THE SNAIL

She goes but softly, but she goeth sure;
  She stumbles not as stronger creatures do:
Her journey's shorter, so she may endure
  Better than they which do much further go.

She makes no noise, but stilly seizeth on
  The flower or herb appointed for her food,
The which she quietly doth feed upon,
  While others range, and gare, but find no good.

And though she doth but very softly go,
  However 'tis not fast, nor slow, but sure;
And certainly they that do travel so,
  The prize they do aim at they do procure.

JOHN BUNYAN

MEETING AT NIGHT

The grey sea and the long black land;
And the yellow half-moon large and low;
And the startled little waves that leap
In fiery ringlets from their sleep,
As I gain the cove with pushing prow,
And quench its speed in the slushy sand.

Then a mile of warm sea-scented beach;
Three fields to cross till a farm appears;
A tap at the pane, the quick sharp scratch
And blue spurt of a lighted match,
And a voice less loud, through its joys and fears,
Than the two hearts beating each to each!

ROBERT BROWNING

THE FARMER AND THE QUEEN

'She's coming,' the farmer said to the owl.
'Oh, what shall I, what shall I do?
Shall I bow when she comes?
Shall I twiddle my thumbs?'
  The owl asked, 'Who?'

'The Queen, the Queen, the royal Queen –
She'll pass the farm today.
Shall I salute?' he asked the horse.
  The horse said, 'Nay.'

'Shall I give her a gift?' he asked the wren.
'A lovely memento for her to keep?
An egg or a peach or an ear of corn?'
  The wren said, 'Cheap.'

'But should I curtsy or should I cheer?
Oh, here's her carriage now.
What should I do?' he asked the dog.
  The dog said, 'Bow.'

And so he did, and so she passed,
Oh, tra lala lala,
'She smiled, she did!' he told the sheep.
  The sheep said, 'Bah.'

SHEL SILVERSTEIN

WAITING FOR THE BARBARIANS

What are we waiting for, assembled in the forum?

    The barbarians are due here today.

Why isn't anything going on in the senate?
Why are the senators sitting there without legislating?

    Because the barbarians are coming today.
    What's the point of senators making laws now?
    Once the barbarians are here, they'll do the legislating.

Why did our emperor get up so early,
and why is he sitting enthroned at the city's main gate,
in state, wearing the crown?

    Because the barbarians are coming today
    and the emperor's waiting to receive their leader.
    He's even got a scroll to give him,
    loaded with titles, with imposing names.

Why have our two consuls and praetors come out today
wearing their embroidered, their scarlet togas?
Why have they put on bracelets with so many amethysts,
rings sparkling with magnificent emeralds?
Why are they carrying elegant canes
beautifully worked in silver and gold?

Because the barbarians are coming today
and things like that dazzle the barbarians.

Why don't our distinguished orators turn up as usual
to make their speeches, say what they have to say?

Because the barbarians are coming today
and they're bored by rhetoric and public speaking.

Why this sudden bewilderment, this confusion?
(How serious people's faces have become.)
Why are the streets and squares emptying so rapidly,
everyone going home lost in thought?

Because night has fallen and the barbarians haven't come.
And some of our men just in from the border say
there are no barbarians any longer.

Now what's going to happen to us without barbarians?
Those people were a kind of solution.

C. P. CAVAFY

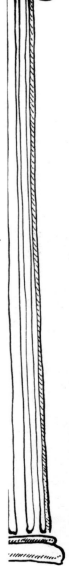

AND MY HEART SOARS

The beauty of the trees,
the softness of the air,
the fragrance of the grass,
  speaks to me.

The summit of the mountain,
the thunder of the sky,
the rhythm of the sea,
  speaks to me.

The faintness of the stars,
the freshness of the morning,
the dew drop on the flower,
  speaks to me.

The strength of fire,
the taste of salmon,
the trail of the sun,
and the life that never goes away,
  they speak to me.

And my heart soars.

CHIEF DAN GEORGE

SPARROW

He's no artist:
His taste in clothes is more
dowdy than gaudy.
And his nest – that blackbird, writing
pretty scrolls on the air with the gold nib of his beak,
would call it a slum.

To stalk solitary on lawns,
to sing solitary in midnight trees,
to glide solitary over grey Atlantics –
not for him: he'd rather
a punch-up in a gutter.

He carries what learning he has
lightly – it is, in fact, based only
on the usefulness whose result
is survival. A proletarian bird.
No scholar.

But when winter soft-shoes in
and these other birds –
ballet dancers, musicians, architects –
die in the snow
and freeze to branches,
watch him happily flying
on the O-levels and A-levels
of the air.

NORMAN MacCAIG

AUTUMN MIST

So thick a mist hung over all,
Rain had no room to fall;
It seemed a sea without a shore;
The cobwebs drooped heavy and hoar
As though with wool they had been knit;
Too obvious mark for fly to hit!

And though the sun was somewhere else
The gloom had brightness of its own
That shone on bracken, grass and stone
And mole-mound with its broken shells
That told where squirrel lately sat,
Cracked hazel-nuts and ate the fat.

And sullen haws in the hedgerows
Burned in the damp with clearer fire;
And brighter still than those
The scarlet hips hung on the briar
Like coffins of the dead dog-rose;
All were as bright as though for earth
Death were a gayer thing than birth.

ANDREW YOUNG

THE FEAST OF CRISPIAN

This day is call'd the feast of Crispian.
He that outlives this day, and comes safe home,
Will stand a-tiptoe when this day is nam'd,
And rouse him at the name of Crispian.
He that shall live this day, and see old age,
Will yearly on the vigil feast his neighbours,
And say 'Tomorrow is Saint Crispian.'
Then will he strip his sleeve and show his scars,
And say 'These wounds I had on Crispian's day.'
Old men forget; yet all shall be forgot,
But he'll remember, with advantages,
What feats he did that day. Then shall our names,
Familiar in his mouth as household words –
Harry the King, Bedford and Exeter,
Warwick and Talbot, Salisbury and Gloucester –
Be in their flowing cups freshly rememb'red.
This story shall the good man teach his son;
And Crispin Crispian shall ne'er go by,
From this day to the ending of the world,
But we in it shall be remembered –
We few, we happy few, we band of brothers;
For he today that sheds his blood with me
Shall be my brother; be he ne'er so vile,
This day shall gentle his condition;
And gentlemen in England now a-bed
Shall think themselves accursed they were not here,
And hold their manhoods cheap whiles any speaks
That fought with us upon Saint Crispin's day.

WILLIAM SHAKESPEARE

THE PTARMIGAN

The ptarmigan is strange,
As strange as he can be;
Never sits on ptelephone poles
Or roosts upon a ptree.
And the way he ptakes pto spelling
Is the strangest thing pto me.

ANONYMOUS

OLD SHEPHERD'S PRAYER

Up to the bed by the window, where I be lyin',
Comes bells and bleat of the flock wi' they two children's clack.
Over, from under the eaves there's the starlings flyin',
And down in yard, fit to burst his chain, yapping out at Sue I
  do hear young Mac.

Turning around like a falled-over sack
I can see team ploughin' in Whithy-bush field and meal carts
  startin' up road to Church-Town;
Saturday arternoon the men goin' back
And the women from market, trapin' home over the down.

Heavenly Master, I wud like to wake to they same green places
Where I be know'd for breakin' dogs and follerin' sheep.
And if I may not walk in th' old ways and look on th' old faces
I wud sooner sleep.

CHARLOTTE MEW

CA' THE YOWES TO THE KNOWES

Ca' the yowes to the knowes,
Ca' them whare the heather growes,
Ca' them whare the burnie rowes,
   My bonnie dearie.

Hark, the mavis' evening sang
Sounding Clouden's woods amang;
Then a-faulding let us gang,
   My bonnie dearie.

We'll gae down by Clouden side,
Thro' the hazels spreading wide,
O'er the waves, that sweetly glide
   To the moon sae clearly.

Yonder Clouden's silent towers,
Where at moonshine midnight hours,
O'er the dewy bending flowers,
   Fairies dance sae cheary.

Ghaist nor bogle shalt thou fear;
Thou'rt to love and heaven sae dear,
Nocht of ill may come thee near,
   My bonnie dearie.

Fair and lovely as thou art,
Thou hast stown my very heart;
I can die – but canna part,
   My bonnie dearie.

ROBERT BURNS

THE MOTH'S PLEA

I am a disappointment
And much worse.
You hear a flutter, you expect a brilliance of wings,
Colours dancing, a bright
Flutter, but then you see
A brown, bedraggled creature
With a shamefaced, unclean look
Darting upon your curtains and clothes,
Fighting against the light.
I hate myself. It's no wonder you hate me.

I meddle among your things,
I make a meal out of almost any cloth,
I hide in cupboards and scare
Any who catch me unaware.
I am your enemy – the moth.

You try to keep me away
But I'm wily and when I do
Manage to hide, you chase me, beat me, put
Horrible-smelling balls to poison me.
Have you ever thought what it's like to be
A parasite,
Someone who gives you a fright,
Who envies the rainbow colours of the bright
Butterflies who hover round flowers all day?
O please believe that I do understand how it feels
To be awake in and be afraid of the night.

ELIZABETH JENNINGS

I, TOO, SING AMERICA

I am the darker brother.
They send me to eat in the kitchen
When company comes.
But I laugh,
And eat well,
And grow strong.
Tomorrow
I'll sit at the table
When company comes
Nobody'll dare
Say to me,
'Eat in the kitchen'
Then.

Besides, they'll see how
Beautiful I am
And be ashamed, –
I, too, am America.

LANGSTON HUGHES

MY BONNY BLACK BESS

Dick Turpin bold! Dick, hie away,
Was the cry of my pals, who were startled, I guess,
For the pistols were levelled, the bullets whizzed by,
As I leapt on the back of Black Bess.
Three Officers mounted, led forward the chase,
Resolv'd in the capture to share;
But I smil'd on their efforts, tho' swift was their pace,
As I urg'd on my bonny Black Mare.
So when I've a bumper, what can I do less,
    Than the memory drink of my bonny Black Bess?

Hark away, hark away! still onward they press,
As we saw by the glimmer of morn,
Tho' many a mile on the back of Black Bess,
That night I was gallantly borne;
Hie over, my pet, the fatigue I must bear
Well clear'd! never falter for breath,
Hark forward, my girl, my bonny Black Mare,
We speed it for life or for death.
But when I've a bumper, what can I do less,
    Than the memory drink of my bonny Black Bess?

The spires of York now burst on my view,
But the chimes, they were ringing her knell,
Halt! Halt! my brave mare, they no longer pursue,
She halted, she staggered, she fell!
Her breathing was o'er, all was hushed as the grave,
Alas! poor Black Bess, once my pride,
Her heart she had burst, her rider to save,
For Dick Turpin, she lived, and she died.

Then the memory drink of my bonny Black Bess,
Hurrah for poor bonny Black Bess!

ANONYMOUS

HINTS ON PRONUNCIATION FOR FOREIGNERS

I take it you already know
Of tough and bough and cough and dough?
Others may stumble, but not you
On hiccough, thorough, laugh and through?
Well done! And now you wish perhaps
To learn of these familiar traps?

Beware of heard, a dreadful word,
That looks like beard and sounds like bird,
And dead: it's said like bed, not bead,
For Goodness' sake, don't call it deed!
Watch out for meat and great and threat,
They rhyme with suite and straight and debt.

A moth is not a moth in mother
Nor both in bother, broth in brother,
And here is not a match for there,
Nor dear and fear for bear and pear,

And then there's does and rose and lose –
Just look them up: and goose and choose,

And cork and front and word and ward
And font and front and word and sword.
And do and go and thwart and cart –
Come, come, I've hardly made a start!
A dreadful language? Man Alive,
I'd mastered it when I was five.

ANONYMOUS

AUTUMN BIRDS

The wild duck startles like a sudden thought,
And heron slow as if it might be caught;
The flopping crows on weary wing go by,
And greybeard jackdaws, noising as they fly;
The crowds of starlings whizz and hurry by
And darken like a cloud the evening sky;
The larks like thunder rise and suther round
Then drop and nest in the stubble ground;
The wild swan hurries high and noises loud,
With white necks peering to the evening cloud.
The weary rooks to distant woods are gone;
With length of tail the magpie winnows on
To neighbouring tree, and leaves the distant crow,
While small birds nestle in the hedge below.

JOHN CLARE

CHRISTMAS WISE

All I **want** fe christmas is world peace
I **don't want** loads a food dat I really can't eat
All I **want** fe christmas is a long holiday
An a house in Jamaica where I can stay.
I **don't want** kisses under mistletoe from
Sloppy people I don't know,
I **won't** be putting out nu stocking cos
I **don't** wear de tings,
I **won't** be cutting down nu christmas trees,
I like dem living.

All I **want** fe christmas is dis planet for ever
Fully complete wid its ozone layer
All I **want** fe christmas is friends and ...
No more records from Status Quo,
I **don't want** a white christmas an I bet
We'll get nu more of dem cos of de Greenhouse effect,
An I **reckon** at christmas we create too much waste
Maybe a green christmas is more to my taste.
All I **want** fe christmas is sum honesty
About de wisdom of christmas
An how it should be
All I **want** fe christmas is clean air,
but I reckon I won't get none

BENJAMIN ZEPHANIAH

HAVE YOU EVER SEEN

Have you ever seen a sheet on a river bed?
Or a single hair from a hammer's head?
Has the foot of a mountain any toes?
And is there a pair of garden hose?

Does the needle ever wink its eye?
Why doesn't the wing of a building fly?
Can you tickle the ribs of a parasol?
Or open the trunk of a tree at all?

Are the teeth of a rake ever going to bite?
Have the hands of a clock any left or right?
Can the garden plot be deep and dark?
And what is the sound of the birch's bark?

ANONYMOUS

THE BURIAL OF SIR JOHN MOORE AFTER CORUNNA

Not a drum was heard, not a funeral note,
　　As his corse to the rampart we hurried;
Not a soldier discharged his farewell shot
　　O'er the grave where our hero we buried.

We buried him darkly at dead of night,
　　The sods with our bayonets turning,
By the struggling moonbeam's misty light
　　And the lanthorn dimly burning.

No useless coffin enclosed his breast,
 Not in sheet or in shroud we wound him;
But he lay like a warrior taking his rest
 With his martial cloak around him.

Few and short were the prayers we said.
 And we spoke not a word of sorrow;
But we steadfastly gazed on the face that was dead,
 And we bitterly thought of the morrow.

We thought, as we hollow'd his narrow bed
 And smooth'd down his lowly pillow,
That the foe and the stranger would tread o'er his head,
 And we far away on the billow!

Lightly they'll talk of the spirit that's gone,
 And o'er his cold ashes upbraid him –
But little he'll reck, if they let him sleep on
 In the grave where a Briton has laid him.

But half of our heavy task was done
 When the clock struck the hour for retiring;
And we heard the distant and random gun
 That the foe was sullenly firing.

Slowly and sadly we laid him down,
 From the field of his fame fresh and gory;
We carved not a line, and we raised not a stone,
 But we left him alone with his glory.

CHARLES WOLFE

MAN AND DOG

They're first there when the library opens,
shuffling, snuffling, her nose to his tread.
   He stops to wheeze.
She shrugs herself down like a rug in a skip.
She stretches out across the heating vent
   and steams her fleas.

A space clears. Only he doesn't wince
at her smell. Only she could love his.
   They're last to go – where
no one knows. I saw them in the park
at dawn. She crouched, just a glance
   to check he's there.

Then sleeked her ears and went swingeing
off to leave a huge dark O around him
   scuffed in the dew,
the way pigeons circle, swerving, homing
round the loft you never see, each sweep
   losing a few.

PHILIP GROSS

254

QUEEN NEFERTITI

Spin a coin, spin a coin.
  All fall down;
Queen Nefertiti
  Stalks though the town.

Over the pavements
  Her feet go clack.
Her legs are as tall
  As a chimney stack;

Her fingers flicker
  Like snakes in the air,
The walls split open
  At her green-eyed stare;

Her voice is thin
  As the ghosts of bees;
She will crumble your bones,
  She will make your blood freeze.

Spin a coin spin a coin,
  All fall down,
Queen Nefertiti
  Stalks through the town.

ANONYMOUS

THE CHILDREN AND SIR NAMELESS

Sir Nameless, once of Athelhall, declared:
'These wretched children romping in my park
Trample the herbage till the soil is bared,
And yap and yell from early morn till dark!
Go keep them harnessed to their set routines:
Thank God I've none to hasten my decay;
For green remembrance there are better means
Than offspring, who but wish their sires away.'

Sir Nameless of that mansion said anon:
'To be perpetuate for my mightiness
Sculpture must image me when I am gone.'
– He forthwith summoned carvers there express
To shape a figure stretching seven-odd feet
(For he was tall) in alabaster stone,
With shield, and crest, and casque, and sword complete:
When done a statelier work was never known.

Three hundred years hied; Church-restorers came,
And, no one of his lineage being traced,
They thought an effigy so large in frame
Best fitted for the floor. There it was placed,
Under the seats for schoolchildren. And they
Kicked out his name, and hobnailed off his nose;
And, as they yawn through sermon-time, they say,
'Who was this old stone man beneath our toes?'

THOMAS HARDY

AN ACCOMMODATING LION

An Athlete, one vacation,
Met a Lion in privation
On a desert where the lion-food was rare.
The Lion was delighted
That the Athlete he had sighted,
But the Athlete wished that he had been elsewhere.

The Athlete dared not fight him,
And he recalled an item
That was published in some journal he had read,
Of a lion that retreated,
Disheartened and defeated,
When an unarmed hunter stood upon his head.

On this hint from print extracted
The Athlete promptly acted,
And brandished both his shoe-heels high in air.
Upon his feat amazing
The Lion sat a-gazing,
And studied the phenomenon with care.

Said the Lion: 'This position
Is quite against tradition,
But I'll gladly eat you any way you choose;
Inverted perpendicular
Will do – I'm not particular!'
He finished him, beginning with his shoes.

TUDOR JENKS

NOVEMBER

The leaves are fading and falling,
   The winds are rough and wild,
The birds have ceased their calling,
   But let me tell you, my child,

Though day by day, as it closes,
   Doth darker and colder grow,
The roots of the bright red roses
   Will keep alive in the snow.

And when the Winter is over,
   The boughs will get new leaves,
The quail come back to the clover,
   And the swallow back to the eaves.

The robin will wear on his bosom
   A vest that is bright and new,
And the loveliest way-side blossom
   Will shine with the sun and dew.

The leaves to-day are whirling,
   The brooks are dry and dumb,
But let me tell you, my darling,
   The Spring will be sure to come.

There must be rough, cold weather,
   And winds and rains so wild;
Not all good things together
   Come to us here, my child.

So, when some dear joy loses
    Its beauteous summer glow,
Think how the roots of the roses
    Are kept alive in the snow.

ALICE CARY

THE COMMON AND THE GOOSE

The law locks up the man or woman
Who steals the goose from off the common
But leaves the greater felon loose
Who steals the common from the goose.

ANONYMOUS

THE SHARK

A treacherous monster is the Shark
He never makes the least remark.

And when he sees you on the sand,
He doesn't seem to want to land.

He watches you take off your clothes,
And not the least excitement shows.

His eyes do not grow bright or roll,
He has astounding self-control.

He waits till you are quite undrest,
And seems to take no interest.

And when towards the sea you leap,
He looks as if he were asleep.

But when you once get in his range,
His whole demeanour seems to change.

He throws his body right about,
And his true character comes out.

It's no use crying or appealing,
He seems to lose all decent feeling.

After this warning you will wish
To keep clear of this treacherous fish.

His back is black, his stomach white,
He has a very dangerous bite.

LORD ALFRED DOUGLAS

THE CATS OF KILKENNY

There were once two cats of Kilkenny,
Each thought there was one cat too many;
So they fought and they fit,
And they scratched and they bit,
Till, excepting their nails
And the tips of their tails,
Instead of two cats, there weren't any.

ANONYMOUS

YOUNG LOCHINVAR

O, young Lochinvar is come out of the west,
Through all the wide Border his steed was the best,
And save his good broadsword he weapons had none;
He rode all unarmed, and he rode all alone.
So faithful in love, and so dauntless in war,
There never was knight like the young Lochinvar.

He stayed not for brake, and he stopped not for stone,
He swam the Eske river where ford there was none;
But, ere he alighted at Netherby gate,
The bride had consented, the gallant came late:
For a laggard in love, and a dastard in war,
Was to wed the fair Ellen of brave Lochinvar.

So boldly he entered the Netherby Hall,
Among bride's-men and kinsmen, and brothers and all:
Then spake the bride's father, his hand on his sword
(For the poor craven bridegroom said never a word),
'O come ye in peace here, or come ye in war,
Or to dance at our bridal, young Lord Lochinvar?'

'I long wooed your daughter, my suit you denied;
Love swells like the Solway, but ebbs like its tide –
And now I am come, with this lost love of mine
To lead but one measure, drink one cup of wine.
There are maidens in Scotland more lovely by far,
That would gladly be bride to the young Lochinvar.'

The bride kissed the goblet; the knight took it up,
He quaffed off the wine, and he threw down the cup.
She looked down to blush, and she looked up to sigh,
With a smile on her lips and a tear in her eye.
He took her soft hand, ere her mother could bar,
'Now tread we a measure!' said young Lochinvar.

So stately his form, and so lovely her face,
That never a hall such a galliard did grace;
While her mother did fret, and her father did fume,
And the bridegroom stood dangling his bonnet and plume;
And the bride-maidens whispered, ''Twere better by far
To have matched our fair cousin with young Lochinvar.'

One touch of her hand, and one word in her ear,
When they reached the hall-door, and the charger stood near;
So light to the croupe the fair lady he swung,
So light to the saddle before her he sprung!
'She is won! we are gone, over bank, bush, and scaur;
They'll have fleet steeds that follow,' quoth young Lochinvar.

There was mounting 'mong Graemes of the Netherby clan;
Fosters, Fenwicks, and Musgraves, they rode and they ran;
There was racing, and chasing, on Cannobie Lee,
But the lost bride of Netherby ne'er did they see.
So daring in love, and so dauntless in war,
Have ye e'er heard of gallant like young Lochinvar?

SIR WALTER SCOTT

AIRMAIL TO A DICTIONARY

Black is the mellow night
Without the black there would be no white.

Black is the pupil of the sky
Putting colour in the sea's skin and earthen sky.

Black is the oil of the engine
On which this whole world is depending.

Black is light years of space
Holding on its little finger this human race.

Black is the colour of ink
That makes the History books we print.

Black is the army. Wars in the night
Putting on the black to hide the white.

Black is the colour of coal
Giving work to the miners and warmth to the cold.

Black is the strip upon my cardcash
That lets me get money from the Halifax.

Black is the shade of the tree
Sharp in definition against inequality.

Black is the eclipse of the sun
Displaying its power to everyone.

Black is the ink from a history
That shall redefine the dictionary

Black on black is black is black is
Strong as asphalt and tarmac is.

Black is a word that I love to see
Black is that, yeah, black is me.

LEMN SISSAY

THE FALLOW DEER AT THE LONELY HOUSE

One without looks in to-night
  Through the curtain-chink
From the sheet of glistening white;
One without looks in to-night
  As we sit and think
  By the fender-brink.

We do not discern those eyes
  Watching in the snow;
Lit by lamps of rosy dyes
We do not discern those eyes
  Wondering, aglow,
  Fourfooted, tiptoe.

THOMAS HARDY

THE EMBARRASSING EPISODE OF LITTLE MISS MUFFET

Little Miss Muffet discovered a tuffet,
    (Which never occurred to the rest of us)
And, as 'twas a June day, and just about noonday,
    She wanted to eat – like the best of us:
Her diet was whey, and I hasten to say
    It is wholesome and people grow fat on it.
The spot being lonely, the lady not only
    Discovered the tuffet, but sat on it.

A rivulet gabbled beside her and babbled,
    As rivulets always are thought to do,
And dragon flies sported around and cavorted,
    As poets say dragon flies ought to do;
When, glancing aside for a moment, she spied
    A horrible sight that brought fear to her,
A hideous spider was sitting beside her,
    And most unavoidably near to her!

Albeit unsightly, this creature politely
    Said: 'Madam, I earnestly vow to you,
I'm penitent that I did not bring my hat. I
    Should otherwise certainly bow to you.'
Though anxious to please, he was so ill at ease
    That he lost all his sense of propriety,
And grew so inept that he clumsily stept
    In her plate – which is barred in Society.

This curious error completed her terror;
   She shuddered, and growing much paler, not
Only left tuffet, but dealt him a buffet
   Which doubled him up in a sailor knot.
It should be explained that at this he was pained:
   He cried: 'I have vexed you, no doubt of it!
Your fist's like a truncheon.' 'You're still in my luncheon,'
   Was all that she answered. 'Get out of it!'

And the *Moral* is this: Be it madam or miss
   To whom you have something to say,
You are only absurd when you get in the curd
   But you're rude when you get in the whey!

GUY WETMORE CARRYL

ONE OLD OX

One old ox opening oysters,
Two toads totally tired
Trying to trot to Tewkesbury,
Three tame tigers taking tea,
Four fat friars fishing for frogs,
Five fairies finding fire-flies,
Six soldiers shooting snipe,
Seven salmon sailing in Solway,
Eight elegant engineers eating exellent eggs;
Nine nimble noblemen nibbling non-pareils,
Ten tall tinkers tasting tamarinds,
Eleven electors eating early endive,
Twelve tremendous tale-bearers telling truth.

ANONYMOUS

REMONSTRANCE WITH THE SNAILS

Ye little snails,
With slippery tails,
Who noiselessly travel
Along this gravel,
By a silvery path of slime unsightly,
I learn that you visit my pea-rows nightly.
Felonious your visit, I guess!
And I give you this warning,
That, every morning,
I'll strictly examine the pods;
And if one I hit on,
With slaver or spit on,
Your next meal will be with the gods.

I own you're a very ancient race,
And Greece and Babylon were amid;
You have tenanted many a royal dome,
And dwelt in the oldest pyramid;
The source of the Nile! – O, you have been there!
In the ark was your floodless bed;
On the moonless night of Marathon
You crawled o'er the mighty dead;
But still, though I reverence your ancestries,
I don't see why you should nibble my peas.

The meadows are yours, – the hedgerow and brook,
You may bathe in their dews at morn;
By the aged sea you may sound your shells,
On the mountains erect your horn;

The fruits and the flowers are your rightful dowers,
  Then why – in the name of wonder –
Should my six pea-rows be the only cause
  To excite your midnight plunder!

I have never disturbed your slender shells;
  You have hung round my aged walk
And each might have sat, till he died in his fat,
  Beneath his own cabbage-stalk:
But now you must fly from the soil of your sires;
  Then put on your liveliest crawl,
And think of your poor little snails at home,
  Now orphans or emigrants all.

  Utensils domestic and civil and social
    I give you an evening to pack up;
But if the moon of this night does not rise
    on your flight,
    Tomorrow I'll hang each man jack up.
  You'll think of my peas and your thievish trick
  With tears of slime, when crossing the Styx.

ANONYMOUS

CORMORANT

Drowned fishermen come back
    As famished cormorants
With bare and freezing webby toes
    Instead of boots and pants.

You've a hook at the end of your nose.
    You shiver all the day
Trying to dry your oilskin pyjamas
    Under the icy spray.

But worst – O worst of all –
    The moment that you wish
For fried fish fingers in a flash
    You're gagged with a frozen fish.

TED HUGHES

CELTIC BENEDICTION

Deep peace of the Running Wave to you.
Deep peace of the Flowing Air to you.
Deep peace of the Quiet Earth to you.
Deep peace of the Shining Stars to you.
Deep peace of the Son of Peace to you.

Index of First Lines

Acknowledgements

The compiler and publisher are grateful for permission to include the following material.

W. H. Auden: 'Roman Wall Blues' from *Twelve Songs* (Faber and Faber Ltd). John Betjeman: 'How to Get On in Society' from *Collected Poems* (John Murray Publishers Ltd 1973). Valerie Bloom: 'Water Everywhere' and 'Lucky Me' from *A Caribbean Dozen* (Walker Books 1994). Edmund Blunden: 'The Idlers' from *The Midnight Skaters* (Bodley Head 1968). By permission of the Peters Fraser & Dunlop Group Ltd. Richard Brautigan: 'The Horse that had a Flat Tyre' from *The Pill Versus the Springhill Mine Disaster* (Dell Publications 1968). R. P. Brett: 'Point of View' from *Poems of the Second World War* (Dent 1985). By permission of the Salamander Oasis Trust. H. D. Carberry: 'Nature' from *New Ships* (Oxford University Press 1975). Charles Causley: 'Six Women', 'Green Man in the Garden' and 'Ballad of the Bread Man' from *Collected Poems* (Macmillan 1992). C. P. Cavafy: 'Waiting for the Barbarians' from *Collected Poems* (Chatto & Windus 1990). Translation copyright © 1975 by Edmund Keeley and Philip Sherrard. Elsie Cawser: 'Salvage Song' from *Poems of the Second World War* (Dent 1985). By permission of the Salamander Oasis Trust. Wang Chien: 'Hearing that His Friend was Coming Back from the War', from *Translations from the Chinese* by Arthur Waley (George Allen & Unwin/HarperCollins Publishers Ltd). Gillian Clarke: 'Anorexic', from *Poetry Nation Review* 1994 (Carcanet Press Ltd). William Clarke: 'Military Cemetery' from *Poems of the Second World War* (Dent 1985). By permission of the Salamander Oasis Trust. Elizabeth Coatsworth: 'Song of the Rabbits Outside the Tavern' from *The Oxford Book of Children's Verse in America* (Oxford University Press 1985); 'On a Night of Snow' from *Poetry Please!* (BBC Publications 1991). Tim Connors: 'The Pantomime' from *Them and Us* (Bodley Head 1993). John Cunliffe: 'Cat Warmth' from *Standing on a Strawberry* (Andre Deutsch 1987). Fred D'Aguiar: 'Mama Dot I' from *Mama Dot* (Random House UK Ltd). Walter de la Mare: 'I Met at Eve'. By permission of the Literary Trustees of Walter de la Mare, and The Society of Authors as their representative. C. P. S. Denholm-Young: 'Dead German Youth' from *Poems of the Second World War* (Dent 1985). By permission of the Salamander Oasis Trust. Berlie Doherty: 'Playgrounds' from *Walking on Air* (HarperCollins Publishers Ltd 1993). Carol Ann Duffy: 'In Mrs Tilscher's Class' from *The Other Country* (Anvil Press Poetry Ltd 1990). Oliver Dunne: 'Uh-Oh' from *Lifelines 2* (Taen House, Dublin). Richard Edwards: 'The Blue Room' from *The Word Party* (Lutterworth Press 1986). U. A. Fanthorpe: 'What the Donkey Saw' from *Poems for Christmas* (1987) © U. A. Fanthorpe, by permission of Peterloo Poets. Elaine Feinstein: 'Dad' from *Poetry Nation Review 1994* (Carcanet Press Ltd). Rose Flint: 'Applemoon' from *Verse Universe 2* (BBC Publications 1993). Rosanne Flynn: 'The City People Meet Themselves' from *Wondercrump Poetry!* (Random House UK Ltd 1994). John Foster: 'It's a Dog's Life' from *Standing on the Sidelines* © John Foster 1995. By permission of Oxford University Press. Chief Dan George: 'And My Heart Soars' © Chief Dan George and Helmut Hirnscholl 1974. By permission of Hancock House Publishing Ltd. Philip Gross: 'Man and Dog' from *Scratch City* (Faber and Faber Ltd 1995). David Harmer: 'Divali' from *Let's Celebrate* (Oxford University Press 1989). Michael Harrison: 'Miss! Sue is Kissing' from *Junk Mail* © Michael Harrison 1993. By permission of Oxford University Press. Seamus Heaney: 'The Railway Children', 'Old Smoothing Iron', 'Glanmore Sonnet V11' and 'Requiem for the Croppies', from *New Selected Poems 1966-1987* (Faber and Faber Ltd 1990). Mary Ann Hoberman: 'Combinations' from *The Oxford of Book Children's Verse in America* (1985). Kevin Horted: 'Who Will Go First?' from *Wondercrump Poetry!* (Random House UK Ltd 1994). Langston Hughes: 'Mother to Son' and 'April Rain Song' from *The Dream Keeper and Other Poems* (Alfred A. Knopf Inc 1932); 'I, Too, Sing America' from *Time* Magazine. Ted Hughes: 'Stickleback' and 'Cormorant' from *The Iron Wolf* (Faber and Faber Ltd); 'Pets' from *Moon Bells and Other Poems* (Chatto & Windus 1978). Both by permission of Faber and Faber. Emyr Humphreys: 'From Father to Son' from *Poetry Please!* (BBC Publications 1991). Randall Jarrell: 'Bats' from *The Bat Poet* (Michael di Capua Books / HarperCollins Publishers) ©1963, 1965 by Randall Jarrell. Permission granted by Rhoda Weyr Agency, NY. Elizabeth Jennings: 'Holidays at Home', 'Old People' and 'The Moth's Plea' from *Poets in Hand* (Penguin Books 1985). Brendan Kennelly: 'Eily Kilbride' from *The Book of Judas* (Bloodaxe Books 1991). By permission of Bloodaxe Books. Liz Lochhead: 'The Choosing' from *Dreaming Frankenstein and Collected Poems* (Paragon Books 1984). Edward Lowbury: 'Prince